GRUNDLAGE DEUTSCH 2

Fundamentals of German

Jessie G. McGuire

Walter G. O'Connell High School, Copiague, NY (retired)

Joseph Castine

Northport High School, Northport, NY (retired)

AMSCO SCHOOL PUBLICATIONS, INC.
315 HUDSON STREET / NEW YORK, NY 10013

Cover design by A Good Thing, Inc.

Please visit our Web site at:
www.amscopub.com

When ordering this please specify *either* **R 64 W** *or*
GRUNDLAGE DEUTSCH 2: FUNDAMENTALS OF GERMAN

ISBN   978-1-56765-408-0

NYC Item   56765-408-X

Copyright © 2007 by Amsco School Publications, Inc.

Printed in the United States of America

1 2 3 4 5 6 7 8 9 10   12 11 10 09 08 07 06

Preface

Grundlage Deutsch 2 is designed as a review of the material covered in a typical second-level German course. It offers learners a chance to review, practice and strengthen their understanding of the German language within communicative contexts. Vocabulary has been limited to basic second-year language, so that *Grundlage Deutsch 2* may be used independently or as a supplement to any basal text.

ORGANIZATION

Grundlage Deutsch 2 consists of 18 chapters, each organized around a single major grammar concept. The base concept is explained succinctly and clearly, illustrated with usage examples, followed by relevant practice exercises for the learner, and then expanded upon. Each expansion explanation follows the same pattern of explanation, examples, and practice exercises. Chapters start with clear introductions to the new concept and expand in small increments until the required functions of the second-level German related to this concept have been introduced, illustrated and practiced.

VOCABULARY AND GRAMMAR

Grundlage Deutsch 2 is not a vocabulary enrichment workbook. Its goal is to offer students of any ability level an opportunity to strengthen their understanding and mastery of the functions needed to communicate in German. The book works with a limited, intermediate core of vocabulary, which was chosen after reviewing several current German texts. The vocabulary is used and recycled into different situational contexts throughout the book. A German-English vocabulary list and numerous grammar charts are included for easy reference.

EXERCISES

Each grammar explanation is followed by a series of exercises. Exercises are based on communicative situations and develop a "story" throughout the chapter. They begin with simple recognition activities and scaffold toward more complex tasks. They progress from easy to more difficult in small, manageable steps that students can easily handle.

FLEXIBILITY

Grundlage Deutsch can be used successfully whether students are working independently, in small learning groups, or in a classroom situation. Each chapter focuses on a single, or a few related grammar concepts. The vocabulary is limited to basic second-year lists, and the extensive table of contents allows learners to identify readily where explanations and exercises relevant to their needs can be found. It can be used independently or with little or no extra preparation as a classroom supplement to any basal level-two German text.

Mastering communicative functions gives learners confidence and a firm basis on which to continue building their knowledge of German. *Grundlage Deutsch 2* cements the essential skills necessary for mastery of level two and increases students' communicative abilities. Its gradual progression from simple to complex, review of previously learned concepts, clear explanations, and transparent organization make it ideal whether used as a classroom tool, a remedial tool, or an enrichment tool. We wish all learners *Viel Glück* as they work through the exercises in *Grundlage Deutsch 2* and look forward to welcoming everyone to level three.

Jessie McGuire and Joseph Castine

Contents

CHAPTER 1

Present Tense
Expressions of Future Time
Giving Commands
Giving Suggestions

1. Formation of the Present Tense

In German, the stem of the verb is formed by dropping the final *–en* (or *–n* if there is no *–en*) from the infinitive.

The present tense is formed by adding the following endings to the verb stem:

PRESENT TENSE CONJUGATION OF WEAK VERBS	
SINGULAR	PLURAL
ich besuche – e *I visit, I do visit, I am visiting*	**wir besuch – en** *we visit, we do visit, we are visiting*
***du besuch – st** *you (informal) visit, do visit, are visiting*	**ihr besuch – t** *you (informal) visit, do visit, are visiting*
****er, sie, es besuch – t** *he, she, or it visits, does visit, is visiting*	**sie besuch – en** *they visit, they do visit, they are visiting*
Sie besuch – en *you (formal) visit, do visit, are visiting*	

NOTE:

*If the verb stem already ends in *–s* or *–ß*, only a *–t* is added in the *du* form of the verb.

**If the verb stem ends in *–t*, *–d*, or two consonants followed by an *–n*, an *–e* is added before the *–st* or *–t* ending in the *du*, *ihr*, or *er/sie/es* forms. This makes the resulting verb easier to pronounce.

ÜBUNG A | **Ferien in Österreich.** You are on vacation in Austria with your family. Using the word prompts, write a postcard to your friends at home telling them about the experience.

EXAMPLE: wir / jeden Tag / im See / schwimmen.   **Wir schwimmen jeden Tag im See.**

1. ich / jeden Morgen / durch den Wald / reiten

---

2. Mutti und Vati / in der Sonne / sitzen / und / lesen

_____

3. das Restaurant / oft / leckere Pommes frites / servieren

_____

4. Rudi und ich / abends / oft / ins Kino / gehen

_____

5. wir / nächsten Donnerstag / nach Hause / fliegen

_____

ÜBUNG B   **Vatis Einladung.** While in Austria, you have become acquainted with a summer school group. Your father has invited you and your new friends on an outing to München next weekend. Collect ideas on what you all like to do there. Use the word _gern_ (or _gerne_) to convey enjoyment of the activity. In this exercise _du_ refers to you yourself, not a friend.

EXAMPLE: Horst / Museen / besichtigen   Horst besichtigt gern(e) Museen.

1. du und dein Vater / in guten Restaurants / essen

_____

2. Axel / in dem olympischen Schwimmbad / baden

_____

3. die ganze Gruppe / in die Sporthalle / gehen

_____

4. du / einen Tee / mit Antje / im Englischen Garten / trinken

_____

5. Dein Bruder und deine Schwester / zu Hause / bleiben

_____

ÜBUNG C   **Telefonanrufe.** Not all your friends were there when you were discussing what to do in the city. Call those who might also go and ask what they enjoy.

EXAMPLE: Egon / in der Jugendherberge / übernachten
           Egon, **übernachtest du gern(e)** in der Jugendherberge?

1. Gerlinde / in die Oper / gehen

_____

2. Max und Moritz / im Tierpark / fotografieren

_____

3. Frau Berger / Schlösser / besichtigen

_____

4. Ava / die neue Mode in den Kaufhäusern / anschauen

_____

5. dein Freund Heller und seine Mutter / zu Hause / bleiben und arbeiten

_____

2.   The Present Tense of Stem Vowel Change Verbs

Certain verbs change their vowel in the _du_ and the _er/sie/es_ forms before adding the personal endings. (See chart below). These verbs must be memorized.

For a complete list of commonly used strong verbs, see page 201 in the appendix.

There are three common stem vowel changes:

_a_ becomes _ä_	**fallen, er fällt**	_fall_	**fahren, er fährt**	_drive, ride_
	schlafen, er schläft	_sleep_	**tragen, er trägt**	_wear, carry_
_e_ becomes _i_	**essen, er isst**	_eat_	**geben, er gibt**	_give_
	helfen, er hilft	_help_	**sprechen, er spricht**	_speak_
	nehmen, er nimmt	_take_	**vergessen, er vergisst**	_forget_
_e_ becomes _ie_	**sehen, er sieht**	_see_	**lesen, er liest**	_read_

CONJUGATION OF STEM-CHANGE VERBS							
SINGULAR				PLURAL			
ich	fahr-e	helf-e	les-e	wir	fahr-en	helf-en	les-en
du	fähr-st	hilf-st	*lies-t	ihr	fahr-t	helf-t	les-t
er, sie, es	fähr-t	hilf-t	**lies-t	sie	fahr-en	helf-en	les-en
	Sie	fahr-en	helf-en	les-en			

*If the verb stem already ends in –s, the _du_-form (normally –st) only adds a –t.
**If the verb stem ends in –t, –d, or two consonants followed by an –n, an –e is added before the –st or –t ending

---

ÜBUNG D | **Wer tut was gern?** You friend Horst made a list of what some of your other friends like to do, but he got everything mixed up. Complete the sentences from the notes he sent you.

EXAMPLE: Hanna / durch die Stadt / gern laufen
Hanna **läuft gern** durch die Stadt.

Hanna	sprechen	gern durch die Stadt
Maria	fahren	gern Pizza
Horst	essen	gern mit der U-Bahn
Mercedes	lesen	gern alle Plakaten
Jakob	ansehen	gerne mit Touristen
Renee	laufen	gerne die alten Kirchen

1. _____

2. _____

3. _____

4. _____

5. _____

ÜBUNG E | **Unser Ausflugsvideo.** You are going to make a video of your excursion to München. Use the story-board to write the narration for the video.

EXAMPLE: Norma fährt mit der Straßenbahn.

1. Nastasja

_____

2. Niels

_____

3. Manuela

_____

4. Marcus

_____

5. Leah

_____

CONJUGATION OF THE VERB **SEIN** — TO BE			
SINGULAR		PLURAL	
ich bin	_I am_	**wir sind**	_we are_
du bist	_you (informal) are_	**ihr seid**	_you (informal) are_
er, sie, es ist	_he, she, or it is_	**sie sind**	_they are_
Sie sind _you (formal) are_			

CONJUGATION OF THE VERB **HABEN** — TO HAVE			
SINGULAR		PLURAL	
ich habe	_I have_	**wir haben**	_we have_
du hast	_you (informal) have_	**ihr habt**	_you (informal) have_
er, sie, es hat	_he, she, or it has_	**sie haben**	_they have_
Sie haben _you (formal) have_			

3.   The Present Tense of the Auxiliary Verbs _sein_ and _haben_

The verb _sein_ and _haben_, like their English counterparts "to be" and "to have", are strong (irregular) and change form depending upon what or whom is being discussed (see tables above).

ÜBUNG F   **Wo bist du?** You and your Austrian friends had fun with your new digital camera. Everyone dressed up as if they were in a different world city and took pictures. Then you had to guess where they were supposed to be. Use the verb _sein_ and the following cities in your answers.

Cuernavaca in Mexico – Glasgow in Schottland – Shanghai in China – Moskau in Russland – Paris in Frankreich – Skagway in Alaska

Example: Ich **bin** in China.

1. Er

_____

2. Sie

_____

3. Wir

_____

4. Du

_____

5. Sie

_____

ÜBUNG G **Letzte Fragen vor der Abreise.** You are getting ready for the trip to München. Your father asks you if you have the things you need. You answer in the positive.

EXAMPLE: deinen Pulli   Hast du deinen Pulli?   Ja, ich habe **meinen** Pulli.

1. deine Tasche _____

2. deinen Schirm _____

3. dein Geld _____

4. dein Mittagsbrot _____

5. deine Fahrkarte _____

ÜBUNG H **Der Ausflug.** Your friends have all brought something to school that they are taking with them on the trip. Using the elements involved, create sentences describing what they have when they arrive at school.

EXAMPLE: Meine Freundin Anika hat ein Reisebuch.

meine Freundin Anika	haben	eine Tasche.
du		ein Reisebuch
Markus und Jasmin		eine Landkarte
ihr		die Fahrkarten
Sie		das Geld
ich		eine Kamera

1. _____

2. _____

3. _____

4. _____

5. _____

ÜBUNG I **Was wir mitnehmen.** Your classmates brought some things to school to show what they are taking on the trip. There was some confusion returning them, so you call Janna to ask if everyone has his or her own articles back. When talking to Janna, make sure you remember to put the direct objects in the accusative case.

EXAMPLE: Karl / sein Rucksack   Janna, hat Karl **seinen** Rucksack?

1. Maria / ihr Reisebuch _____

2. Marta / ihr Stadtplan _____

3. Mechthild / ihr Fahrplan _____

4. Du, Janna / deine Reisetasche _____

5. Herr Marzipan / die Fahrkarten _____

4.   Separable Prefixes in the Present Tense

A preposition is often used to complete the meaning of a verb. "I'll pick you up." or "He's driving away." In German the completer is attached to the beginning of the verb, i.e. *abholen*. It starts the infinitive, and is then separated and sent to the end of its utterance (clause, phrase or sentence) when conjugated in a sentence.

Below is a list of several separable prefix verbs. If the verb is strong, the third person singular vowel-change form has also been given.

abfahren, fährt... ab	*depart*
anfangen, fängt... an	*begin*
anhaben, hat... an	*have on*
ankommen	*arrive*
anrufen	*call*
anziehen	*put on (clothing), pull on*
aufhören	*stop doing (something)*
aufmachen	*open*
aufräumen	*clean up*
aufstehen	*get up, stand up*
ausgehen	*go out*
aussehen	*look (appearance)*
einkaufen	*buy*
einladen, lädt... ein	*invite*
fernsehen, sieht... fern	*watch TV*
herkommen	*come from*
hingehen	*go to*
mitbringen	*bring with, bring along*
mitgehen	*go with, go along*
mitkommen	*come along, come with*
mitnehmen, nimmt... mit	*take with, take along*
nachkommen	*come after*
vorhaben, hat... vor	*have planned*

vorlesen,	
liest... vor	*read aloud*
weggehen	*go away*
zuhören	*listen to*
zumachen	*close*
zurückgehen	*go back*

NOTE: German is modular, like building blocks. When faced with the need for a new word, rather than invent something, German will usually combine two or more familiar words or add prefixes and suffixes to an existing one. Because of this, students often comprehend more at an earlier level than with many other languages. You are encouraged to use separable prefixes creatively. The risk of making an error is minimal and the resulting German is much more fluid and precise.

ÜBUNG J   **Das Interview.** Rudi has been given the opportunity to interview a rock star for the school newspaper. Maja and Robert are excited and accompany him on the trip. Complete the report that Maja wrote about the trip by building verbs with a prefix and stem and then using them in the story. Cross out the verbs as you use them.

zurück	~~kommen~~
~~an~~	hören
an	gehen
aus	haben
mit	sehen
zu	fahren

Rudi __kommt__ in München ___an___. Er _____ einen schwarzen Anzug _____,

weil er ein Interview hat. Maja findet, er _____ gut _____. Maja und Robert

_____ auch zum Interview _____. Sie warten auf Rudi im Wartezimmer. Im

Wartezimmer vom Interviewer _____ sie Rockmusik _____. Nach dem Interview

gehen alle drei ins Café und essen Kuchen. Rudi schaut auf seine Uhr und sagt: „Es ist vier

Uhr. Wir _____ jetzt _____."

5.   Using the Present Tense to Indicate Future Tense

When combined with an adverb or adverbial phrase that implies futurity, the present tense may also be used to express future actions. The list below contains the most common adverbial phrases indicating a time in the future.

sofort	*immediately*
bald	*soon*
später	*later*
heute	*today*
morgen	*tomorrow*
übermorgen	*the day after tomorrow*
heute Morgen / Nachmittag / Abend	*this morning, afternoon or evening*
am Montag . . .	*on Monday . . .*
morgen früh	*tomorrow morning*
morgen Nachmittag / Abend	*tomorrow afternoon or evening*
nächste Woche	*next week*
nächsten Monat	*next month*
nächstes Jahr	*next year*
in einer Stunde / Woche	*in an hour or in a week*
in einem Monat / Jahr	*in a month or in a year*

EXAMPLE: **Wir fahren nächsten Samstag nach München.**   *We're going to Munich next Saturday.*

NOTE: English often places the location before the time in a sentence. "We're going to the movies tomorrow." German modifiers are always placed in TMP order: time (when) – manner (how) – place (where).

EXAMPLE: **Wir gehen morgen mit meinem Vater ins Kino.**
                              time   manner   place

ÜBUNG K   **Unsere Pläne.** Use the adverbs or phrases above to write a short story about what you and you friends will be doing in München.

EXAMPLE: Nächstes Wochenende fahren wir nach München.

1. _____

2. _____

3. _____

4. _____

5. _____

ÜBUNG L   **Was machen wir?** Some of your friends are not really sure about what you are doing next weekend. Build questions with the sentence elements. Make sure you put the modifiers in TMP order (time, manner, place).

EXAMPLE: wir / nächstes Wochenende / nach München / fahren
                      Fahren wir nächstes Wochenende nach München?

1. Rudi / auch / in die Stadt /am Samstag / mitkommen

___

2. wir / später / ins Kino / gehen

___

3. wir / um eins / im Restaurant / gemütlich / essen

___

4. die ganze Gruppe /in die Sporthalle / am Samstag Nachmittag / mitgehen

___

5. wir / am Sonntag / zurückfahren

___

6. Giving Instructions, Directions and Commands

When giving a command either in English or German the word "you" is seldom used.

Come here. Turn at the corner. Don't stay out too late. Please help me.

In German, there are three different command forms, depending upon the relationship of the speaker with the person(s) who is (are) to perform the action. Note that all commands are punctuated with an exclamation point.

kommen   (du) **Komm(e)** zu mir! *Come to me.*   **lesen** *(du) **Lies** das Buch!

(ihr) **Kommt zu mir!   (ihr) **Lest** das Buch!

(Sie) **Kommen Sie** zu mir!   (Sie) **Lesen Sie** das Buch!

anfangen   (du) **Fang** jetzt **an**!   *Begin now.*

(ihr) **Fangt jetzt **an**!

(Sie) **Fangen Sie** jetzt **an**!

*If the verb stem requires an *e* to *ie* or *e* to *i* vowel change, the changed vowel is used for the *du* imperative form. The *a* to *ä* vowel change is not carried over into the imperative.

Lies das Buch! *Read the book.*   **Sieh mich an!** *Look at me.*

**If the verb stem ends in –*d*, –*t*, or two consonants followed by an –*n*, add –*et* to the second person plural imperative rather than just –*t*. This rule is consistent throughout German.

Öffnet die Tür! *Open the door.*   **Arbeitet zu zweit!** *Work in pairs.*

| ÜBUNG M | **Aufgaben für den Ausflug.** You are making a list of tasks you're assigning your friends for the upcoming trip. Write out your requests. |

EXAMPLE: Fritz / der Stadtplan / bitte / mitbringen
        Fritz, bring bitte den Stadtplan mit!

1. Herr Marzipan / die Fahrkarten / bitte / kaufen

   _____

2. Gerd und Maya / die Videokamera / nicht / bitte / vergessen

   _____

3. Anna / so spät / nicht / bitte / kommen

   _____

4. Marianne / unsere Klassenliste / bitte / aufschreiben

   _____

5. Jakob / die Wettervorhersage / bitte / anschauen

   _____

7. Giving a Suggestion

Rather than a command or instruction, the speaker may wish to either include herself in the group activity, or make a casual suggestion rather than a demand. This is accomplished by using the contraction "let's" in English: "Let's go shopping." In German, the *wir* form of the verb and inverted word order is used: *Gehen wir einkaufen*.

Gehen wir! *Let's go.*   **Essen wir!** *Let's eat!*   **Hören wir jetzt   auf!** *Let's stop now.*

ÜBUNG N | **Vorschläge.** While thinking about the upcoming trip, you create a list of suggestions for the group. Write them in a note before you forget them.

EXAMPLE: durch den Park gehen   Gehen wir durch den Park!

1. ein Museum besichtigen

   _____

2. Pizza essen

   _____

3. einen Film sehen

   _____

4. mit der U-Bahn fahren

   _____

5. Sonntag um 6.30 Uhr aufstehen

   _____

ÜBUNG O | **Eine Email.** Use the sentence elements below to write an e-mail to your sister about the planned trip to München.

EXAMPLE: Wir / fahren / mit der Bahn   Wir fahren mit der Bahn.

1. Rudi / kaufen / Fahrkarten

2. Emma / mitbringen / eine Videokamera

3. Dirk / essen / viel Pizza

4. Herr Marzipan / einladen / Frau Schultz

5. Marissa / mitfahren / auch

ÜBUNG P   **Unser Klassenausflug.** Now you are ready for the trip. Write a story to your pen pal about what you are planning to do. Use the present tense and adverbs to indicate your plans for the weekend. Write at least eight sentences using at least six of the suggested verbs.

fahren	gehen	mitkommen
essen	laufen	mitbringen
lesen	sehen	anschauen

EXAMPLE: Wir fahren mit der Bahn nach München.

ÜBUNG Q | **Austauschprogramm.** The return trip. This fall your school is hosting a GAPP (German American Partnership Program) exchange. The German visitors will be staying in your town for three weeks. Write what you are planning to do with them and when, using destinations within your area.

_____

_____

_____

_____

_____

_____

_____

_____

_____

CHAPTER 2

Plural Nouns
Articles
Possessive Adjectives

1.   Plural Nouns

Pluralizing a noun in English is easy. With very few exceptions only an –s is added to the singular. In German, all nouns form their plurals differently. Like its gender, the plural must be memorized with each noun. The definite article of all plural nouns is *die*.

The last word in a compound word is the one which is pluralized.

das Wurstbrot, die Wurstbrote

2.   Patterns of Plural Nouns

There is no rule for pluralizing nouns, but there are recurring patterns. The examples below provide vocabulary one might encounter during a stay in a city or in the country.

a. Add an –*e* (often pluralizes *der*-words and *das*-words)

das Geschäft, die Geschäfte	**der Dom, die Dome**
das Meer, die Meere	**der Kiosk, die Kioske**
das Ruderboot, die Ruderboote	**der Ozean, die Ozeane**
das Schreibwarengeschäft, die Schreibwarengeschäfte	**der Schnellimbiss die Schnellimbisse**
das Zelt, die Zelte	**der Waldweg, die Waldwege**
der Berg, die Berge	

b. Add an *umlaut* and an –*e* (often pluralizes monosyllabic words with *a*, *u*, or *o*)

der Campingplatz die Campingplätze	**der Marktplatz, die Marktplätze**
der Fluss, die Flüsse	**der Schlafsack, die Schlafsäcke**
der Friedhof, die Friedhöfe	**der Strand, die Strände**
der Gasthof, die Gasthöfe	**der Supermarkt, die Supermärkte**
	die Stadt, die Städte

c. Add an –*er* (often pluralizes monosyllabic *das*-words)

das Feld, die Felder	**das Geld, die Gelder**

d. Add an *umlaut* and an *–er* (often pluralizes *der*-words and *das*-words)

das Dorf, die Dörfer	das Rathaus, die Rathäuser
das Hallenbad, die Hallenbäder	das Schwimmbad,
das Hochhaus, die Hochhäuser	die Schwimmbäder
das Kaufhaus, die Kaufhäuser	das Tal, die Täler
das Krankenhaus, die	das Wohnhaus, die Wohnhäuser
Krankenhäuser	der Bauernhof, die Bauernhöfe
das Postamt, die Postämter	der Wald, die Wälder

e. Add an *–n* (often pluralizes *die*-words ending in *–e, –ie, –er* or *–el*)

der/die See, die Seen	die Oper, die Opern
die Ampel, die Ampeln	die Schule, die Schulen
die Drogerie, die Drogerien	die Stadthalle, die Stadthallen
die Jugendherberge, die	die Tankstelle, die Tankstellen
Jugendherbergen	die Wiese, die Wiesen
die Kirche, die Kirchen	die Wüste, die Wüsten

f. Add an *–en* (often pluralizes *die*-words ending in *–schaft, – heit, -ung, –ei,* or *–keit*)

die Bäckerei, die Bäckereien	die Metzgerei, die Metzgereien
die Bank, die Banken	die Sehenswürdigkeit, die
die Bibliothek, die Bibliotheken	Sehenswürdigkeiten
die Buchhandlung, die	die Wohnung, die Wohnungen
Buchhandlungen	

g. Add an *–nen* (pluralizes *die*-words ending in *–in*)

die Ärztin, die Ärztinnen	die Lehrerin, die Lehrerinnen

h. No change from singular (often pluralizes *der / das-* words or ending in *–el* or *–er*)

das Gebäude, die Gebäude	der Hügel, die Hügel
das Theater, die Theater	der Krankenwagen, die
der Bürgermeister, die	Krankenwagen
Bürgermeister	

i. Add an *umlaut* to the stressed vowel

der Garten, die Gärten	der Laden, die Läden
der Hafen, die Häfen	die Mutter, die Mütter

j. Add an *–s* (often pluralizes contemporary words of foreign origin)

das Hotel, die Hotels	der Friseursalon, die
das Internetcafé, die Internetcafés	Friseursalons
das Kino, die Kinos	der Park, die Parks
das Restaurant, die Restaurants	der Zoo –s

| ÜBUNG A | **Das Plurallied.** You're writing a class song to sing on the train. It's one of those designed to drive those not singing crazy. It's called **das Plurallied**. You start with 12 and sing your way back down to one. You're writing it to the tune of "Twinkle, Twinkle Little Star". Create the next 11 items to add into the song. Add anything that will make your song fun and interesting to sing. |

Strophe eins:
Wir machen eine Klassenfahrt. Unterwegs sehen wir zwölf Zelte.
Was macht ihr jetzt ? Eine Klassenfahrt.
Was seht ihr unterwegs? Zwölf Zelte sehen wir.
Wir machen eine Klassenfahrt. Wer möchte heute mit uns kommen?

Strophe zwei:
Wir machen eine Klassenfahrt. Wir sehen zwölf Zelte und elf . . . . unterwegs.

EXAMPLE: Wir sehen zwölf Zelte und elf Hügel unterwegs.

11. Wir sehen zwölf Zelte und elf Hügel unterwegs. _____

10. _____

9. _____

8. _____

7. _____

6. _____

5. _____

4. _____

3. _____

2. _____

1. _____

3.   Definite Articles

All nouns are masculine (*der*), feminine (*die*) or neuter (*das*). Regardless of the gender, the plural article is *die*. Complete charts for both the definite and indefinite articles are reproduced below to use as reference.

DEFINITE ARTICLES				
	SINGULAR			PLURAL
	MASCULINE	FEMININE	NEUTER	
NOMINATIVE	der	die	das	die
DATIVE	dem	der	dem	den
ACCUSATIVE	den	die	das	die

4.   Indefinite Article and *kein/keine/kein*

The indefinite article *ein/eine/ein* is translated as "a" or "an." The ending is determined by its GNC, i.e. the gender of the noun it modifies (masculine, feminine or neuter), the number (singular and plural) and the case (nominative, dative or accusative).

The negation *kein/keine/kein* is translated as "no", "none" or "not any". *Kein* takes the same endings as *ein*.

INDEFINITE ARTICLES				
	SINGULAR			PLURAL
	MASCULINE	FEMININE	NEUTER	
NOMINATIVE	ein	eine	ein	keine
DATIVE	einem	einer	einem	keinen
ACCUSATIVE	einen	eine	ein	keine

ÜBUNG B   **Ich sehe . . . .** Your class is traveling together in a train and you're playing *"Ich sehe . . ."* One of your classmates will tell you what they see and you reply by saying either that you do see the article, or that you don't. Write your answers on your own, and then take a poll in the class to see whether your answer was in the majority or the minority.

EXAMPLE: die Kirche   Ich sehe eine Kirche.   or Ich sehe keine Kirche.

1. die Bibliothek

_____

2. das Postamt

_____

3. der Fluss

_____

4. die Jugendherberge

_____

5. das Rathaus

_____

5.   Possessive Adjectives

The following words show possession and are used to modify a noun. They take the same endings as *ein/eine/ein* (see chart below.)

POSSESSIVE ADJECTIVES			
SINGULAR		PLURAL	
PRONOUN	POSSESSIVE ADJECTIVE	PRONOUN	POSSESSIVE ADJECTIVE
ich	mein *my*	wir	unser *our*
du	dein *your*	ihr	euer *your*
er	sein *his*	sie	ihr *their*
sie	ihr *her*		
es	sein *its*		
Sie	Ihr *your*		

*The middle *e* is optional when adding endings to *unser* or *euer*. You may use **unsere** or *unsre/euere* or *eure*.

ÜBUNG C   **Ist das deine Tasche?** You have returned from your field trip to München and must return some objects to their owners. Ask if the following things belong to the person or persons named. You are on a du basis with all those for whom first names are given.

EXAMPLE: Holger – die Tasche   Holger, ist das deine Tasche?

1. Danica – die Kamera

_____

2. Eike und Emilio – der Stadtplan

_____

3. Herr Marzipan – das Buch

_____

4. Herr und Frau Marzipan – die Ansichtskarten

_____

5. Holger – der Regenschirm

_____

ÜBUNG D   **Das Fundbüro.** Some things have still not been claimed by their owners. You call up various students to identify the owners of the remaining things.

EXAMPLE: Rudi – sein Fußball   Rudi, habe ich deinen Fußball?

1. Maria – das Fotoalbum

_____

2. Adam – die Tasche

_____

3. Herr Schultz – der Schirm

_____

4. Basil und Babette – die CDs

_____

ÜBUNG E   **Das Klassenfundbüro.** You also have a list of things that some of your classmates are missing. Since you seem to be the appointed "finder", you call your classmates to see if they have something that doesn't belong to them.

EXAMPLE: (You call Markus) Günter - der Schal   Markus, hast du seinen Schal?
                                                  Markus, do you have his scarf?

1. (You call Rudi) Johann – der Pulli

_____

2. (You call Petra und Peter) Camille und Carlo – das Reisebuch

_____

3. (You call Johanna) Petra – der CD-Spieler

_____

4. (You call Herr Marzipan) Angelika – das Bilderbuch von München

_____

ÜBUNG F   **Alles ok.** Everything seems straightened out. You just go through the items in your mind to reassure yourself that everyone has what they brought.

EXAMPLE: Petra / Stadtplan von München   Ja, Petra hat ihren Stadtplan von München.

1. Rudi / Kamera _____

2. Johanna / Regenschirm_____

3. Gerd und Gerlinde / Rucksäcke _____

4. ich / Postkarten _____

5. du / Bilderbuch von München _____

ÜBUNG G **Deine Checkliste.** Do you have the following items that were needed for the
trip? Write whether you have one of them or not. Vary your answers.

EXAMPLE: Ich habe ein Reisebuch.
Ich habe kein Reisebuch.

1. _____

2. _____

3. _____

4. _____

5. _____

| **ÜBUNG H** | **Freiluftkonzert.** You're planning a trip to an open air concert next weekend. It's only two hours away, but you've decided to spend the night at a local campground and come back the following day. Make a list of whom you will invite and what each of them will bring. Make sure you use words such as her, his, their, etc. |

_____

_____

_____

_____

_____

_____

_____

_____

_____

_____

_____

_____

_____

_____

_____

_____

_____

_____

CHAPTER 3

Nouns and Pronouns
Es gibt

1. Subject Nouns

In German, all nouns have gender. They are either masculine (*der*), feminine (*die*) or neuter (*das*).

All nouns also have number. They are either singular or plural.

Nouns used in a sentence also have case. They are nominative, dative or accusative depending upon their use in the sentence. Many students prefer to think of these three attributes as the GNC of a noun. Establishing the GNC of the nouns in a sentence determines exactly what endings to use on their articles or on any adjectives that modify them. (See tables on page 206.)

The subject of the sentence is the person or thing performing the action of the verb. Subject nouns use the nominative case.

ÜBUNG A | **Gefühlskarten.** You've been given a deck of "emotion" playing cards. Before you can play your card you have to describe it. In order to lay down a card you have to write one sentence describing who's on it and how that person is (or those people are) feeling. In a second sentence you have to write the reason why you think they feel that way.

EXAMPLE: Der Mann ist traurig.   Er kann seine Frau nicht finden.

1. _____

_____

2. _____

_____

3. _____

_____

4. _____

_____

5. _____

_____

2.   Predicate Nouns

Often there are two nouns in the sentence that mean the same thing. One is the subject. The other follows a linking verb, called a verb of being, and means the same thing as the subject. These nouns are called predicate nouns and also take the nominative case. In the sentence below, _das Tier_ is the subject. _Ein Elefant_ is the predicate noun.

Das Tier ist ein Elefant. _The animal is an elephant._

Mein Onkel ist der Trompetenspieler im Kieler Blasquartett.

My uncle is the trumpet player in the Kiel Brass Quartet.

ÜBUNG B   **Ordne zu.** It's another card game. This time you can only lay down pairs of cards. As you lay down your pair, announce why you think those two pictures go together to form a pair.

EXAMPLE: Die Knackwurst ist eine Wurst.

das Pferd	die Blume
die Rose	das Tier
der Spinat	das Obst
die Limo	das Gemüse
der Apfel	das Getränk
die Knackwurst ◄──────► die Wurst

1. _____

2. _____

3. _____

4. _____

5. _____

3. Direct Object Nouns

The direct object receives the action of the verb and is always in the accusative case. The tables below show the accusative endings for the definite and indefinite articles.

DEFINITE ARTICLES			
	SINGULAR		PLURAL
	MASCULINE	FEMININE	NEUTER	
NOMINATIVE	der	die	das	die
DATIVE	dem	der	dem	den
ACCUSATIVE	den	die	das	die

INDEFINITE ARTICLES			
	SINGULAR		PLURAL
	MASCULINE	FEMININE	NEUTER	
NOMINATIVE	ein	eine	ein	keine
DATIVE	einem	einer	einem	keinen
ACCUSATIVE	einen	eine	ein	keine

NOTE: How does one identify the function of each noun in a sentence? The easiest way is to find the verb first. In the first sentence on page 26, for example, the verb is **machen**, *to make*. Who or what is making? The 11th grade. That answer is the subject of the sentence and is in the nominative. What are they making? A class trip. That is the direct object and in the accusative case. The subject performs the action of the verb and the direct object receives the action of the verb.

Unsere Schulklasse macht im Mai eine Klassenfahrt nach Marbach.

Our class is taking a class trip in May to Marbach.

Die elfte Klasse besichtigt das Schiller Geburtshaus und den alten Marktplatz.

The 11th grade is visiting Schiller's birthplace and the old market square.

ÜBUNG C | **Marbacher Besuch.** You're making plans for your upcoming class trip to Marbach. Make a list of the things you can do when you're there.

EXAMPLE: der Marktplatz / sehen   Ich kann den Marktplatz sehen.

1. das Rathaus / besichtigen

   _____

2. ein Film / sehen

   _____

3. eine Weisswurst / in Bad Cannstatt / essen

   _____

4. ein Kaffee / im Café zum Schillermuseum / trinken

   _____

5. eine Disco / am Neckar / finden

   _____

ÜBUNG D | **Andenken kaufen.** You've got an hour to do some shopping before you head home from Marbach. There are some souvenirs you want to buy for your family. Fill in the list once you have decided what you are buying each person.

EXAMPLE: Für meine Mutter kaufe ich eine Halskette.

die Halskette - das Bilderbuch – der Mini-Bierkrug – die kleine Kuckucksuhr – die Spielkarten – das Schweizer Messer

1. Für meinen Bruder Rolf kaufe ich _____

2. Für meine Schwester Karin kaufe ich _____

3. Für meine Freundin bringe ich _____

4. Für meine Großeltern kaufe ich _____

5. Für meinen Freund Paul kaufe ich _____

4.   *Es gibt*

In German, the introductory "there is" and "there are" are expressed in German using *es gibt* (literally, "it gives") followed by the accusative case.

Es gibt 13 Schüler und einen Lehrer in der 11. Klasse.
There are 13 students and one teacher in the 11th grade.

Wie viele Museen gibt es in Marbach?
How many museums are there are in Marbach?

| ÜBUNG E | **Meine Stadt.** You are sending an e-mail to your pen pal telling her about your town. Make a list of at least six places/things that exist in your town. Refer to the list of nouns in Chapter 2 if you need vocabulary help. |

EXAMPLE: Es gibt einen Fußballplatz.

1. _____

2. _____

3. _____

4. _____

5. _____

6. _____

5.   Subject Pronouns

A pronoun replaces a noun in a sentence. Like the noun, the pronoun changes form depending upon its use in the sentence. If it is the subject or predicate noun, then the nominative pronoun is used.

SUBJECT AND DIRECT OBJECT PRONOUNS					
	NOMINATIVE	ACCUSATIVE		NOMINATIVE	ACCUSATIVE
I	**ich**	**mich**	*we*	**wir**	**uns**
you (informal)	**du**	**dich**	*you (informal)*	**ihr**	**euch**
he (masculine)	**er**	**ihn**			
she (feminine)	**sie**	**sie**	*they*	**sie**	**sie**
it (neuter)	**es**	**es**			
you (formal)	**Sie**	**Sie**	*you (formal)*	**Sie**	**Sie**

ÜBUNG F   **Nett sein.** You have decided to say something nice each day to the people you know. Write some sentences you might say to the following people.

EXAMPLE: Herr Marzipan / nett   Herr Marzipan, Sie sind sehr nett.

1. Petra / sein / intelligent

   _____

2. Frau Engels / aussehen / gut

   _____

3. Johann / sein / sportlich

   _____

4. Mario und Markus /sein /die besten Schüler

   _____

5. Mutti / spielen / Basketball / gut

   _____

ÜBUNG G   **Etwas Nettes sagen.** You've decided what nice things you want to say to your friends and family the next time you see them. You're discussing it with your grandmother and telling her about your decisions. Use the sentences you wrote above to create your conversation with her.

EXAMPLE: Herr Marzipan / nett   Er ist sehr nett.

1. _____

2. _____

3. _____

4. _____

5. _____

6.   Pronouns Replacing Inanimate Objects

A pronoun does not always replace the name of a person. When it replaces the name of a thing, it must have the same GNC as the noun it replaces. In the example below, *der See* is masculine, singular and nominative. The pronoun referring to it must also be MSN, i.e., *er*.

Der See? Er ist riesig groß!   *The lake? It's huge!*

In the following sentence the situation is similar. *Mantel* is MSA. The pronoun replacing it must also be masculine and accusative. *Meinen Mantel* is therefore replaced with the MSA pronoun *ihn*.

Ich kann meinen Mantel nicht finden. Siehst du ihn irgendwo?

I can't find my coat. Do you see it anywhere?

Had the word been *die Sonne*, the German would say that "she" is shining brightly today, not it. The pronoun must always have the same GNC as the noun it replaces.

Die Halskette ist so schön. Danke. Ich mag sie sehr.

The necklace is so pretty. Thanks. I like it very much.

ÜBUNG H   **Eine Email über deine Stadt.** You are writing an e-mail to your pen pal telling him about your town. Use one of the suggested adjectives / adverbs in your descriptions. The two final sentences should be about your real town.

EXAMPLE: das Rathaus - sein / klein / groß   Das Rathaus? Es ist klein.

1. die Schule - sein / modern / alt

   _____

2. der Sportplatz - sein / schön / nicht sehr

   _____

3. das Postamt - liegen / in der Nähe / weit weg

   _____

4. die Bibliothek - besitzen / nicht / sehr viele / Bücher

   _____

5. _____

6. _____

ÜBUNG I   **Es gibt in meiner Stadt...** Now write to your pen pal and tell her what other places are in your town, what you think of some of them and why. Add at least two places to the list.

EXAMPLE: das Kino   Es gibt ein Kino. Ich habe es nicht gern. Es ist zu klein.

1. die Kirche / sehr schön

   _____

   _____

2. die Schwimmhalle / zu klein

   _____

   _____

3. das Jugendzentrum / zu alt

_____

_____

4. der Supermarkt / sehr sauber

_____

_____

5. der Park / sehr groß

_____

_____

6. _____

_____

7. _____

_____

NOTE: There are two more cases other than nominative and accusative that will be addressed in the course of this book. It is important to remember that a pronoun always replaces a noun or refers back to a noun. It must match that noun in gender and number. The case will be determined by its use in the sentence.

ÜBUNG J   **Der Video-Ablaufplan.** You are going to make a video about your town for your pen pals in Germany. First you need to write a story board. Use the pictures to get started and then continue for at least 4 sentences. Be sure to write down what is in your town and something about it. Use pronouns.

EXAMPLE: Es gibt einen Sportplatz. Er ist zu klein. Ich habe ihn nicht gern.

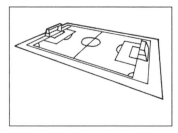

1. _____

2. _____

3. _____

4. _____

5. _____

6. _____

7. _____

8. _____

ÜBUNG K	**Stadt der Zukunft.** It's the year 3000 and you're describing where you live for your great grandchildren, who may or may not even live on the same planet. Be creative. Lifestyles and institutions within a community have changed a lot. Describe where you live, what's there, what you like, what you don't like. Illustrate your description. Vary your writing style and word order. Make sure you use nouns and pronouns so that your German sounds natural, not like a grammar exercise.

_____

_____

_____

_____

_____

_____

_____

_____

_____

_____

_____

_____

_____

_____

CHAPTER 4
Indirect Object Nouns and Pronouns
Expressing Comfort and Discomfort

1. Indirect Object Nouns

The indirect object states to whom, for whom, or from whom something is done.

Der Museumsdirektor zeigt uns die Bilder von Rembrandt.
The director of the museum is showing us the paintings of Rembrandt.

Kaufst du deiner Mutter etwas?   *Are you buying your mother anything?*

Geben Sie uns bitte zwei Käseplatten!   *Please give us two cheese platters.*

The indirect object is always in the dative case.

a. The Dative Definite Article

The dative definite article changes depending upon whether it is used before a masculine, feminine, neuter or plural noun. (See chart below.)

Der Museumsdirektor erzählt den Schülern die Lebensgeschichte von Schiller.

The museum director is telling the students Schiller's life story.

Er zeigt der elften Klasse Schillers Geburtshaus.

He shows the eleventh grade Schiller's birth house.

Zuerst liest er seinen jungen Gästen ein Gedicht von Schiller vor.

First he reads a poem by Schiller aloud to his young guests.

Dann gibt er ihnen eine Tour durch das Haus.

Then he gives them a tour through the house.

The following chart shows the definite articles in the dative, as well as in the nominative and accusative you already know.

THE DEFINITE ARTICLES			
	SINGULAR		PLURAL
	MASCULINE	FEMININE	NEUTER	
NOMINATIVE	der	die	das	die
DATIVE	dem	der	dem	den
ACCUSATIVE	den	die	das	die

b. The Indefinite Article in the Dative Case

The following chart shows the indefinite articles in the dative, as well as in the nominative and accusative you already know.

THE INDEFINITE ARTICLES				
	SINGULAR			PLURAL
	MASCULINE	FEMININE	NEUTER	
NOMINATIVE	ein	eine	ein	meine
DATIVE	einem	einer	einem	meinen
ACCUSATIVE	einen	eine	ein	meine

NOTE: *Kein* and the possessive adjectives (*mein, dein, sein, ihr, unser, euer* and *Ihr*) follow the same pattern as the indefinite article.

| ÜBUNG A | **Briefe, Postkarten und Emails.** You are making a list of relatives to whom you will either send a letter, a postcard or an email while you are on your trip. Which would you choose for the following people? Add two more to the list.

EXAMPLE: mein Vater; Ich schicke meinem Vater eine Postkarte.
Ich schicke meiner Freundin eine E-Mail.

1. meine Mutter_____

2. mein Bruder _____

3. meine Cousine _____

4. _____

5. _____

c. Plural Nouns in the Dative

When using a noun in the dative plural, a final *–n* or an *–en* must be added to the noun unless it already ends in *–n* or *–s*. This is one of the very few times where nouns change in German. In the example below, the plural form *Schüler* receives a final *–n* because it is in the dative.

Im Restaurant bringt der Kellner den Schülern die Speisekarte.

In the restaurant the waiter brings the students the menu.

| ÜBUNG B | **Vorbereitungen.** To help you get ready for the trip to Marbach your teacher has planned a number of activities. Write your pen pal a message telling her what you, your classmates, and your teacher are going to do.

EXAMPLE: Herr Marzipan liest der Klasse ein Gedicht vor.

Herr Marzipan   (vorlesen / zeigen) → (seine Schüler / die Klasse →) → (ein Gedicht / ein Bild von Schiller)

wir	schreiben	die Eltern	eine Einladung per Post
	schicken	unsere Eltern	die Einladungen
ich	bringen	mein Freund	ein Lied
	vorspielen	mein Lehrer	ein Buch über Marbach

1. Herr Marzipan _____

2. Wir _____

3. Wir _____

4. Ich _____

5. Ich _____

ÜBUNG C | **Der Angeber.** Your friend Klaus is nice, but he always feels the need to be the biggest and the best. He tries to top everything anyone else says. You're working on a report with him. Complete the conversation by inserting Klaus' boasts about what he's planning to do. Use the plural wherever possible.

EXAMPLE: Du: Ich lese morgen in einem Buch die Lebensgeschichte von Schiller.
Klaus : Nur in **einem**? Ich lese morgen seine Lebensgeschichte in **drei Büchern**.

Du: Ich telefoniere morgen mit einer Schillerspezialisten.

Klaus : _____

Du : Sie gibt mir dann den Namen von einem guten Buch über Schiller.

Klaus : _____

Du : Ich spreche ja auch am Nachmittag mit einem alten Verwandten von ihm.

Klaus : _____

Du : In meinem Bericht zitiere ich direkt aus einem Schillerwerk (**zitieren** = to quote).

Klaus : _____

Du sagst: Schließlich gebe ich einem Schüler meinen Bericht zu lesen.

Klaus sagt:_____

ÜBUNG D | **Andere machen auch mit.** Another student has written about things that will take place on the Marbach trip, but was only thinking of herself and a friend when she wrote the article. You have to change the underlined parts of the sentences to the plural since the entire class is involved.

EXAMPLE: In Marbach erzählt der Lehrer <u>dem Schüler</u> die Geschichte von Schiller.
In Marbach erzählt der Lehrer den Schülern die Geschichte von Schiller.

1. Herr Marzipan bringt <u>dem Jungen und dem Mädchen</u> einen Stadtplan.

_____

2. Karl liest <u>seinem Freund</u> ein Gedicht von Schiller vor.

_____

3. Marlies kauft <u>ihrem Bruder</u> eine CD von der Stadtkapelle Marbach.

_____

4. Herr Marzipan gibt <u>meinem Klassenkameraden</u> eine Tour.

_____

5. Wir schreiben <u>unserem Vater</u> einen Brief.

_____

2. Indirect Object Pronouns

Just as in English, the pronoun changes in the dative case.

DATIVE CASE PRONOUNS			
SINGULAR		PLURAL	
mir	_me, to me, for me_	**uns**	_us, to us, for us_
dir	_you, to you, for you (informal)_	**euch**	_you, to you, for you (informal)_
ihm	_him, to him, for him_	**ihnen**	_them, to them, for them_
ihr	_her, to her, for her_		
ihm	_it, to it ,for it_		
Ihnen	_you, to you, for you (formal)_		

ÜBUNG E | **Kannst du bitte etwas für mich tragen?** The class is getting ready for the trip. Herr Marzipan gives everyone something to carry.

EXAMPLE: Gerd / der Stadtplan von Marbach   Er gibt ihm den Stadtplan.

1. Marta / die Broschüre von dem Schiller Museum

_____

2. die Zwillinge Gerd und Gerda / der Fahrplan

_____

3. Hansi / das Schilllerbuch

_____

4. Frau Raetzel / die Schülerausweise

_____

5. du / die Fahrkarten

_____

3. Direct/Indirect Object Word Order

German word order is the same as in English. If both direct and indirect object are stated as nouns, the indirect object is mentioned before the direct object.

Die Schüler kaufen ihren Freunden kleine Andenken aus Marbach.

The students buy their friends small souvenirs from Marbach.

| ÜBUNG F | **Eine Einkaufsliste.** You are planning your trip to Marbach and making a list of things you will buy for friends and family. Match the list with the person(s) and write out the sentences.

EXAMPLE: Ich kaufe meinem Onkel einen Stadtplan.

meine Mutter	eine Schilleruhr
mein Vater	ein Buch über Schiller
~~mein Onkel~~	ein Buch über Marbach
meine Tante	~~ein Stadtplan~~
meine Freundin	eine CD von der Stadtkapelle Marbach
die Zwillinge	ein Schillerposter

1. _____

2. _____

3. _____

3. _____

5. _____

If the direct object is a pronoun, it goes before the indirect object regardless of whether the indirect object is a noun or a pronoun.

Gibst du deiner Tante die Schilleruhr? Ja, ich gebe sie meiner Tante.

Are you giving your aunt the Schiller clock? Yes, I am giving it to my aunt.

NOTE: The interrogative for "to whom" or "for whom" is **wem**.

Wem gibst du die Schilleruhr? Deiner Tante? Ja, ich gebe sie ihr.

To whom are you giving the Schiller clock? (To) your aunt? Yes, I'm giving it to her.

Whether in a sentence or sentence fragment, if the noun asks or answers the question "to whom?", "for whom?" or "from whom?" without using a preposition, then it must be in the dative. In the above sentence: *wem, deiner Tante* and *ihr* are all indirect objects in the dative case. The word "to" is already included in the dative. You do not have to add it in again.

| ÜBUNG G | **Ich zeige euch...** You're asking Herr Marzipan what he will be showing you in Marbach. What does he answer? |

EXAMPLE: die Alexanderkirche   Ja, ich zeige sie euch.

1. die Marktstraße_____

2. der Burgplatz _____

3. die Altstadt _____

4. das Dorfmuseum _____

5. das Glockenspiel_____

6. der Torturm _____

7. das Schiller-Denkmal_____

8. Schillers Geburtshaus _____

| ÜBUNG H | **Geschenke.** Your brother wants to know what you are buying for your friends and relatives. Answer his questions using a direct object pronoun in the answer. |

EXAMPLE: Wem gibst du den Stadtplan?   Ich gebe ihn meinem Onkel.

1. Wem gibst du die Schilleruhr? (Freund)

_____

2. Wem gibst du das Schillerposter? (Freundin)

_____

3. Wem gibst du das Buch über Schiller? (Zwillinge)

_____

4. Wem gibst du die CD? (Mutter)

_____

5. Wem gibst du das Buch über Marbach? (Vater)

_____

4.   Expressing Comfort or Discomfort Using the Dative

Wie geht es Ihnen? Wie geht es dir/euch?	*How are you?*
Es geht mir gut.	*I'm fine.*
Es ist mir heiß / kalt / warm / kühl.	*I'm hot / cold / warm / cool.*
Es tut mir weh.	*I hurt. It hurts (me).*
Mein (or Der) Kopf tut mir weh.	*My head hurts. (singular)*
Meine (or Die) Augen tun mir weh.	*My eyes hurt. (plural)*

Note: German is changing. *Die Augen tun mir weh.* (literally, "the eyes hurt to me") or *Ich habe mir das Bein gebrochen.* (literally, "I broke to myself the leg") used to be the only acceptable way to say that your eyes hurt, or that you had broken your leg. Today either: *Mein Bauch tut mir weh.* ("my stomach hurts") or *Der Bauch tut mir weh* (literally, "the stomach hurts me") is acceptable. Both options require the dative.

ÜBUNG I	**Rollenspiel.** You have to role play in a game with your friends. Each of you gets a picture and pretends to be the person with a discomfort. Write out the sentences for the cards.

EXAMPLE: Mein Kopf tut mir weh.

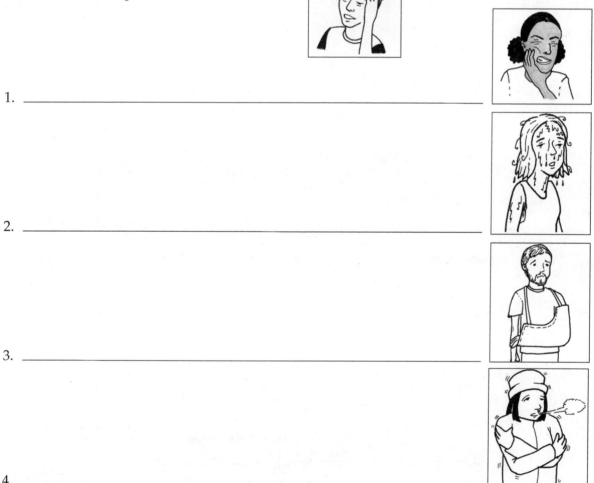

1. _____

2. _____

3. _____

4. _____

5. _____

ÜBUNG J | **Eine Grippe.** Imagine that you are in Germany and go to the doctor because you are not feeling well. You think you have *eine Grippe* (flu) because you ache all over. The doctor asks you where it hurts and you tell him.

EXAMPLE: Kopf   Wo tut es dir weh?   Mein (or Der) Kopf tut mir weh.

1. Augen _____

2. Hals _____

3. Muskeln _____

4. Brust _____

5. Ohren _____

ÜBUNG K | **Ein Gespräch.** Gerrit and Gabi are having a conversation, but you can only hear his side. How do you think Gabi is responding? Use the dative in your answers.

EXAMPLE: Gerrit: Was machst du heute?
          Gabi: Ich kaufe meinen Verwandten Geschenke.

1. Gerrit: Was kaufst du deinem Vater?

   Gabi: _____

2. Und deiner Schwester?

   Gabi: _____

3. Gerrit: Toll! Was gibst du deiner Mutter?

   Gabi: _____

4. Gerrit: Schade. Was tut ihr weh?

   Gabi: _____

5. Gerrit: _____

   Gabi: Oh ja, vielleicht eine CD von einer Jenaer Gruppe.

ÜBUNG L   **Wie bitte?** In your message to your pen pal you either forgot some people or your pen pal didn't understand. He writes back asking for clarification. You write him back and explain.

EXAMPLE: Deine Schwester? Tasche
Meine Schwester? Was kaufe ich für sie? Ich kaufe ihr eine Tasche.

1. Deine Mutter? Taschenuhr

_____

2. Dein Bruder? Schweizer Messer

_____

3. Marika? Buch

_____

4. Deine Freundin? Blumen

_____

5. Dein Vater? CD von Heino

_____

ÜBUNG M   **Ein Dieb.** The dative can also be used to mean "from whom." Imagine you're a high class thief in an exclusive resort area. Make a list of what you would steal from whom. The resort can be a beach resort, a spa, a ski lodge, etc. The setting might make a difference on what you want to steal and from whom.

NOTE: *Stehlen* is the formal word "to steal." A less formal word is *klauen*.

EXAMPLE: Dem Mann im Boot dort drüben stehle ich seine Scuba-Tauchbrille.
Dem Kind neben ihm klaue ich seine Cola.

1. _____

2. _____

3. _____

4. _____

5. _____

CHAPTER 5

Prepositions
Giving Directions

In German, a preposition expresses a relationship between two things. In the sentences below, both *in* and *mit* are prepositions.

Heute sind wir hier im Schwarzwald.   **Die zehnte Klasse ist mit uns.**

Today we're here in the Black Forest.   *The tenth grade is with us.*

1.   Dative Prepositions

The following prepositions require a dative object.

aus	*out, out of*
außer	*except (for), with the exception of*
bei	*at the home of, near*
mit	*with*
nach	*after, to (with geographic location – **nach Bonn**), toward*
seit	*since (referring to time)*
von	*of, from*
zu	*to, toward, to (with people or institutions –**zur Schule, zum Bäcker**)*
*gegenüber	*across from, opposite*

*gegenüber is a post-preposition. It follows, rather than precedes, its object.

In der Schule sitzt er mir gegenüber.

In school he sits opposite me.

Die Buchhandlung steht in der Goethestraße der Bank gegenüber.

The bookstore is on Goethe Street across from the bank.

NOTE: The contractions *zum (zu dem)* and *zur (zu der)* add variety to a text. Other dative contractions include *vom (von dem)* and *beim (bei dem)*.

ÜBUNG A	**Mein Schultag.** Your friends Hans and Fritz tell you about their day. You want to write a story for your German class. Your teacher has given you some sentence elements. You must add some more.

EXAMPLE: nach / Neustadt / fahren   Fritz fährt nach Neustadt

1. er / zu / die Post / gehen / müssen

   _____

2. Hans / mit / er / gehen

   _____

3. dann / Hans und Fritz / zu / das Kaufhaus / hinlaufen

   _____

4. sie / Tennisbälle / von / eine Verkäuferin in der Sportabteilung / kaufen

   _____

5. der Spielplatz / das Kaufhaus / gegenüber / liegen

   _____

6. sie / von / das Kaufhaus / zu / der Spielplatz / hinüberlaufen

   _____

7. Außer / ein Tennistrainer / niemand / auf dem Spielplatz / sein

   _____

8. sie / eine Stunde Tennis / mit / der Tennistrainer / spielen

   _____

ÜBUNG B	**Morgen.** Hans writes you a quick note to tell you what he is doing tomorrow. He spilled cola on it and some words are illegible. Which prepositions from the dative list are missing?

Ich gehe ____na ch der Schule zu____ Fritz. Dann gehen wir _____m Hallenbad. Wir

gehen ___i___ Franz schwimmen. Das Hallenbad liegt in der Marktstrasse dem Rathaus

_____en_____. N_____ dem Schwimmen essen wir _____i Fritz.

2.   Accusative Prepositions

The following prepositions require an accusative object.

*bis	*until, up to*
durch	*through*
für	*for*

gegen	*against, around or about (referring to time)*
ohne	*without*
um	*at (temporal), around (referring to location)*
**entlang	*along*

*Often *bis* is combined with other prepositions. When that occurs, the noun takes the case governed by the second preposition.

Die Marathonrenner laufen bis zum Erdinger Stadtstadion.

The marathon runners run to the Erdinger City Stadium.

***entlang* is a post-preposition. It follows, rather than precedes, its object.

Ich laufe diese Straße entlang bis zur Bank.

I'll walk along this street up to the bank.

| ÜBUNG C | **Ein Team hat Vorsprung.** Hans and Maria are now talking about the planned Fußball game against Marbach. One of the teams is down one player. Fill in the gaps with the correct prepositions to discover which team will have the disadvantage. |

bis, ~~durch~~, für, gegen, ohne, um, entlang

Wir wollen __durch__ den Stadtpark _____ zum Sportplatz laufen. Wir laufen die Park

Straße _____ _____. _____ vier Uhr spielen wir Fußball

_____ die Mannschaft von Marsbach. Leider spielen wir _____ unseren besten

Spieler. _____ unsere Mannschaft kann das nicht gut sein.

3.   Two-way Prepositions

Some prepositions take either dative or accusative objects depending upon their use in the sentence or phrase. They include:

an	*on, at*	**über**	*over, about,*
auf	*on, on to, up*		*above, across*
hinter	*behind*	**unter**	*under, among*
in	*in, into*	**vor**	*before, in front of*
neben	*next to, near*	**zwischen**	*between*

a. Dative of Place (location)

Two-way prepositions take a dative case object when indicating location, i.e. when they describe where someone or something is.

Die Oper in unserer Stadt ist im Park hinter dem Fluss.

The opera in our city is in the park behind the river.

ÜBUNG D **Mein Zimmer.** You are describing your room to your pen pal. Using the picture write out where each item is in relationship to the other items in the room.

EXAMPLE: die Bücher / das Regal   Die Bücher sind auf dem Regal.

1. die Stereoanlage / der Tisch _____

2. die Uhr / der Computer _____

3. der Fussball / das Bett _____

4. das Bild / die Wand _____

5. die Schuhe / das Bett _____

6. die Lampe / die Ecke _____

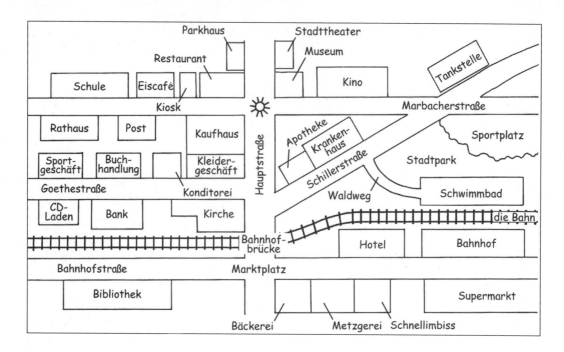

ÜBUNG E   **Eine Kleinstadt in Österreich.** Your classmates will be asking you about the town you visited in Austria. Looking at the map above, write down where certain buildings are in relationship to others. There will be more than one correct way to describe the location of the buildings.

EXAMPLE: das Rathaus / die Post   Das Rathaus ist neben der Post.

1. die Schule / das Rathaus

_____

2. der Stadtpark / der Sportplatz

_____

3. die Buchhandlung / die Konditorei / das Sportgeschäft

_____

4. die Apotheke / die Schillerstrasse

_____

5. die Kirche / die Bank

_____

b. Accusative of Place (movement)

Two-way prepositions take the accusative case when indicating motion towards a goal, i.e., when the prepositional phrase explains where someone or something is going.

Wir gehen zuerst in die Buchhandlung, dann in den Sportladen, und schließlich in das neue Kleidergeschäft.

First we're going to the bookstore, then in the sport store, and finally into the new clothing store.

ÜBUNG F   **Wo geht die Katze hin?** You little cousin sends you a picture story about
where her cat usually goes. Use the pictures to write the story.

gehen – to go **kriechen** – crawl **schleichen** – slink **springen** – jump

EXAMPLE: Die Katze geht **hinter den Sessel**.

1. _____

2. _____

3. _____

4. _____

5. _____

ÜBUNG G | **Wo schläft die Katze?** The cat has finally fallen asleep. Using the same pictures ask your cousin where.

EXAMPLE: hinter / die Couch   Schläft die Katze hinter der Couch?

1. hinter / der Sessel

   _____

2. unter / die Couch

   _____

3. auf / der Tisch

   _____

4. in / das Bett

   _____

5. vor / das Regal

   _____

ÜBUNG H | **Ferienbilder.** You are showing your friends pictures from your vacation. In each picture you and your relatives are standing still, but buses, cars, streetcars, or bicycles are moving near you. Describe the pictures using the same prepositional phrase, once in the dative to show your location, and once in the accusative to show the vehicles' movement toward a goal.

EXAMPLE: ich / in / die Hauptstrasse / stehen   Ich stehe in der Hauptstrasse.
           der Bus / fahren   Der Bus fährt in die Hauptstrasse.

1. ich / auf / die Brücke / stehen _____

   das Auto / fahren_____

2. meine Mutti / neben / das Rathaus / stehen _____

   das Motorrad / fahren_____

3. mein Bruder / vor / der Sportplatz / sitzen_____

   das Rad / fahren _____

4. mein Vater und ich / unter / eine Straßenlampe / stehen_____

   das Moped / fahren_____

5. wir / in dem Stadtpark / stehen _____

   drei Skaters / hineinskaten (sep. prefix hinein•skaten) _____

6. unsere Freundin / vor der Bäckerei / stehen _____

   ein Taxi / fahren_____

7. meine Katze / zwischen / die Tierhandlung und das / Café sitzen_____

   der Roller / fahren _____

| ÜBUNG I | **Besorgungen machen.** Your friends are running errands. Write notes on where they have to go and what they have to do.

EXAMPLE: sie / in / die Goethestrasse / hineinfahren
   Sie fahren in die Goethestrasse hinein.

1. Der CD-Laden / liegen / in / die Goethestraße

   _____

2. Maria / warten / in / der Bahnhof

   _____

3. Maximilian / in / der Bahnhof / hineingehen

   _____

4. Laura / die Hauptstraße / entlang / spazieren

   _____

5. Tilman / in / ein Café / auf / der Marktplatz / sitzen

   _____

4.   Giving Directions

Giving directions is now easy. Objects of a dative preposition are in the dative case regardless of whether they show motion or not.

Fahren Sie geradeaus bis zur Ampel.   *Drive straight ahead until the traffic light.*

Objects of accusative prepositions are always in the accusative case.

Laufen Sie durch den Tunnel und dann über die Brücke.
Walk through the tunnel and then over the bridge.

If the preposition is two-way, then it's either dative or accusative. If the phrase indicates location, the object must be in the dative.

Sie stehen jetzt vor dem Bahnhof.   *You're standing in front of the train station now.*

If the two-way prepositional phrase shows motion towards a goal, then the object must be in the accusative.

Fahren Sie links in die Nohlenstraße ein, dann biegen Sie rechts in das Parkhaus ein.
Drive left onto Nohlenstraße, then turn right into the parking facility.

ÜBUNG J | **Anweisungen zum Sportplatz.** You are standing in front of the train station and ask for directions to the Sportplatz. A policewoman gives you the directions. Trace the route on the map on page 46.

Der Sportplatz? Diese Straße heißt die Bahnhofsstraße. Gehen Sie diese Straße entlang bis zur Hauptstraße. Biegen Sie rechts in die Hauptstraße ein. Dann gehen Sie geradeaus über die Bahnhofsbrücke. Auf der linken Seite sehen Sie die Schillerstraße. Biegen Sie rechts ein. Der Sportplatz ist auf der rechten Seite an der Ecke Schillerstraße und Marburgerstraße.

ÜBUNG K | **Hier bin ich.** You will be calling your friend to give her directions from the train station to the CD-Laden where you will meet her. You have made some notes and must now prepare the directions so that you don't make mistakes.

Anika, du stehst vor _____ Bahnhof und dann gehst du rechts. Du gehst d_____

Bahnhofstrasse entlang bis zu_____ Marktplatz. Hier biegst du rechts in _____

Hauptstrasse. Geh geradeaus über _____ Bahnhofsbrücke. Links siehst du _____

Goethestrasse. Geh links in _____ Goethestrasse und dann geradeaus. Ich stehe auf

_____ linken Seite vor _____ CD-Laden.

ÜBUNG L | **Der arme Waldemar.** Poor Waldemar. He got lost in the city. Combine the elements to create four different places he could be and four where he could go.

über   die Brücke

der Bahnhof

       entlang

auf   die Strasse   durch

       das Stadttheater

der Sportplatz   die Bibliothek   in

vor   hinter   die Schule

der Supermarkt   neben

unter   zu   das Kino

Wo ist Waldemar?

1. _____

2. _____

3. _____

4. _____

Wohin geht Waldemar?

1. _____

2. _____

3. _____

4. _____

ÜBUNG M | **Vom Bahnhof zu mir**. Your friend Karl is arriving at the train station. Send him an e-mail with directions from the train station to the Sportplatz where you will be playing soccer. Model your directions on others in this chapter.

_____

_____

_____

_____

_____

_____

5. Pronoun Objects of Prepositions – The *da-* and *wo-*Constructions

a. Inanimate Pronoun Objects of Prepositions

Prepositions may have a noun or a pronoun object.

Meine Mutter geht mit meinem Bruder ins Kino.

My mother is going with my brother to the movies.

Or "my brother" may be replaced with the pronoun "him":

Meine Mutter geht mit ihm ins Kino.

Up to this point, there is no difference from English. In the case above, the GNC of brother is MSN, so the pronoun is *ihm*. This works only if the pronoun refers to a person or other living thing with a personality.

If the pronoun refers to an inanimate object, i.e., a non-living thing, German attaches *da-* to the beginning of the preposition and eliminates the need for an object. All pronouns use *da-* regardless of their gender, number and case.

Meine Mutter geht mit ihrem Rezept in die Apotheke.

My mother is going to the pharmacy with her prescription.

"With the prescription" is replaced with "with it". There is no need for an additional object of the preposition.

Meine Mutter geht damit in die Apotheke.

My mother is going with it to the pharmacy.

| ÜBUNG N | **Was machst du damit?** Your friend is asking you what is happening to the things you have lying on your bed.

EXAMPLE: Was passiert mit dem DVD von „Herr der Diebe"?
mit / mein Bruder / zu einem Freund / geht
Mein Bruder geht zu einem Freund damit.

1. Und was machst du mit den alten Kleidern?
über / ich / mit meiner Mutter / sprechen / müssen

_____

2. Und mit diesem Stück Leder?
aus / ich / ein Gürtel / machen / wollen

_____

3. Kannst du dieses alte Zelt noch gebrauchen?
ja / mit / in Mai / zelten / gehen / können

_____

4. Behältst du diese alte Reisetasche?
nein / mit / ich / nichts / machen / können

_____

5. Magst du dieses Cornelia Funke Buch?
ja / aber / gegen / du / etwas / haben ?

_____

b. Pronoun Objects of Prepositions that Begin with a Vowel

If the preposition begins with a vowel, *dar-* is added rather than *da*.

Kinobesucher strömen aus dem Rivoli jeden Abend um 22 Uhr.

Moviegoers stream out of the Rivoli every evening at 10 o'clock.

Kinobesucher strömen jeden Abend um 22 Uhr daraus.

Moviegoers stream out of it every evening at 10 o'clock.

| ÜBUNG O | **Siehst du?** You are using the map to tell your fiends about the city. Make notes so that you say everything correctly.

EXAMPLE: Siehst du den Bahnhof? aus / viele Leute / jeden Tag / laufen
Daraus laufen jeden Tag viele Leute.

1. Siehst du den Sportplatz?   auf / wir / am Montag / Fussball / spielen

_____

2. Siehst du den Marktplatz?   auf / es / jeden Samstag / ein Flohmarkt / geben

_____

3. Siehst du die Bibliothek?   es / in / ein Konzert / jeden Monat / geben

_____

4. Siehst du die Wand von der Schule?   an / es / eine schöne Mosaik / geben

_____

5. Siehst du das Rivoli Kino?   in / man / gute Filme / sehen / können

_____

| ÜBUNG P | **Meine Stadt.** Now you are writing a description of your town. You must write something about the features of your town and what happens at the different locations.

EXAMPLE: Das ist unser altes Museum   vor / viele / Touristen / ein Photo / machen
Davor machen viele Touristen ein Foto.

1. Unsere neue Schule ist nur ein Jahr alt.   in / 400 Schüler / jeden Tag / lernen

_____

2. Unsere Uni ist nicht sehr groß   auf / nur / vier tausend Studenten / gehen

_____

3. Der Bahnhof ist sehr alt.   vor / ein Springbrunnen / stehen

_____

4. Unser Stadtpark ist prächtig.   neben / unser großer Sportplatz / liegen

_____

5. Die Bahnhofsbrücke sieht sehr interessant aus.   über / viel Autoverkehr / fahren / und

unter / die Bahn / fahren

_____

6.   Interrogative Pronouns

A pronoun may also replace a noun when asking a question.

Ich möchte bitte Frau Doktor Schneider sehen.   _I'd like to see Dr. Schneider please._
Wen möchten Sie sehen?   _Whom would you like to see?_

The word "who" must be used in the proper case according to its use in the sentence.

THE INTERROGATIVE PRONOUN "WHO"		
NOMINATIVE	**wer**	*who*
DATIVE	**wem**	*whom, to whom, for whom*
ACCUSATIVE	**wen**	*whom*

NOTE: The word "whom" is rapidly disappearing in English. That is not the case in German. If the pronoun is dative or accusative, *wem* or *wen* must be used.

Wer kommt morgen mit uns?	*Who is coming with us tomorrow?*
Wem soll ich meine Fahrkarte geben?	*To whom should I give my ticket?*
Gegen wen rennst du im Marathon?	*Against whom are you running in the Marathon?*

ÜBUNG Q   **Wie bitte?** You are talking on the phone and the connection is bad. Ask for clarification of the statements you hear.

EXAMPLE: Tag Josef, hier spricht ....
            Wer spricht?

1. Ich komme morgen mit ....

   _____ kommst du?

2. Wir spielen Fussball gegen ....

   _____ spielen wir?

3. Du kennst doch .....

   _____ soll ich kennen?

4. ...... kommen auch mit mir.

   _____ kommt auch mit dir?

5. Ich stelle unser Team zusammen. Du hast doch nichts gegen ...., oder?

   _____ soll ich nichts haben?

7.   Interrogatives in Prepositional Phrases

If the interrogative (question word) is in a prepositional phrase, *wem* or *wen* is used if it refers to a person on an animal, i.e., when it translates as "who" or "whom."

Mit wem fahren wir morgen?	*With whom are we riding tomorrow?*
Bei wem wohnst du in Innsbruck?	*With whom are you living in Innsbruck?*

If the interrogative refers to a thing rather than a person, then *wo-* or *wor-* is attached to the beginning of the preposition. There is no further object of the preposition necessary.

Wovon spricht die Professorin morgen? *What is the professor speaking about tomorrow?*

Mit wem spricht er? *With whom is he speaking?*

ÜBUNG R | **Jeopardy.** You're playing the tv game "Jeopardy" with your friends. Create questions to the following answers. Use a *wo(r)* - construction and the following prepositions

durch – für – von – nach – vor

EXAMPLE: Antwort: Eine Gabel (essen)   Frage: Womit essen wir?

1. Antwort: ein Bus (fahren)   Frage: _____

2. Antwort: eine Brille (sehen)   Frage: _____

3. Antwort: die Bibel (sprechen)   Frage: _____

4. Antwort: P (im Alphabet)   Frage: _____

5. Antwort: die Türmatte (liegen)   Frage: _____

ÜBUNG S | **Der Plan.** You are planning a trip into your city on Saturday. Write your pen pal about your plans. Be sure to include where you are going and when. Use adverbs of time and many prepositions.

EXAMPLE: Am Samstag fahren wir in die Stadt. Zuerst gehen wir ins Kino.

_____

_____

_____

_____

_____

_____

_____

CHAPTER 6
Adjective Endings

1. Predicate Adjectives

An adjective describes a person, place or thing. Adjectives following a linking verb are called predicate adjectives and are easy to use in German. They take no endings.

Ich bin intelligent und nett.

I am intelligent and nice.

Das Museum war sehr interessant, aber der Film war langweilig.

The museum was interesting, but the film was boring.

ÜBUNG A	**Mein Held oder meine Heldin.** You and your pen pal are comparing heroes. Write an essay about a person you admire. List at least six good attributes of this person. When you're done, read your sentences to the class. Can they guess whom you've been describing?

EXAMPLE: Er ist sehr intelligent.

1. _____

2. _____

3. _____

4. _____

5. _____

6. _____

Mein Held oder meine Heldin heißt_____

ÜBUNG B	**Meine Schule.** Now you are writing about your school for your pen pal. Once again you should discuss at least six qualities you like about your school.

EXAMPLE: Meine Schule ist sehr klein.

1. _____

2. _____

3. _____

4. _____

5. _____

6. _____

2.   Weak Adjective Endings

Adjectives do not always follow a linking verb. Often they appear before the noun they modify. In that case, endings are added to the adjective depending upon the gender, number and case (GNC) of the noun that it modifies.

Adjectives sandwiched between the definite article (_der/die/das_) and a noun end either in _–e_ or _–en_. The _–e_ and _–en_ are called weak adjectives endings. (See table below.) There are only 5 _–e_ endings; all the others are _-en_.

Kennst du das alte Volkslied „Die schöne Königstochter"?

Do you know the old folk song "The Lovely Princess"?

WEAK ADJECTIVE ENDINGS _following a_ DEFINITE ARTICLE			
	SINGULAR		PLURAL
	MASCULINE	FEMININE	NEUTER	
NOMINATIVE	der alt-e	die alt-e	das alt-e	die alt-en
DATIVE	dem alt-en	der alt-en	dem alt-en	den alt-en
ACCUSATIVE	den alt-en	die alt-e	das alt-e	die alt-en

ÜBUNG C   **Reisetasche packen.** You are packing for your trip and discussing what to take with your friend. She suggests a general category of something you should take, and you decide exactly which one to take by adding at least one adjective.

EXAMPLE: Deine Pullis sind schön. Ja, ich nehme den blauen Pulli mit.

1. Du hast zwei Gürtel. _____

2. Welche Tasche nimmst du?_____

3. Nimmst du ein Buch mit?_____

4. Diese T-Shirts sind lustig. _____

5. Brauchen wir einen Schirm?_____

ÜBUNG D | **Mein Packzettel.** Now it's your turn. Your German class is attending a Sprachfest in a town five hours away. Schools from all over the area are sending teams to participate in the three-day competition. Write a detailed packing list of everything you'll need. Your mother has to identify each item to make sure everything is clean, so make sure you include descriptive adjectives with each item. Write your sentences as:

"Ich nehme den _____en, die _____e, *or* das _____e mit."

_____

_____

_____

_____

_____

_____

_____

_____

_____

_____

3.   Mixed Adjective Endings

Adjectives sandwiched between the indefinite article (*ein/eine/ein, kein,* or a possessive adjective such as *mein* and *dein*) and a noun end in either *–er, –es, –e* or *–en*. These are called mixed adjective endings.

Compare the following table to the weak adjective ending above. The endings are *-en* in all but the same five squares as above.

MIXED ADJECTIVE ENDINGS *following an* INDEFINITE ARTICLE			
	SINGULAR		PLURAL
	MASCULINE	FEMININE	NEUTER	
Nom	ein alt-er	eine alt-e	ein alt-es	meine alt-en
Dat	einem alt-en	einer alt-en	einem alt-en	meinen alt-en
Akk	einen alt-en	eine alt-e	ein alt-es	meine alt-en

Mein, dein, sein, ihr, unser, euer, Ihr and *kein* are all *ein*-words.

Heute ist unser erster Glas-Recycling-Tag, aber ich habe keine leeren Flaschen.
Today is our first bottle recycling day, but I don't have any empty bottles.

NOTE: There are two steps to finding the correct adjective ending.

1. Determine the correct GNC of the noun it modifies

   In the sentence above the nouns are *Glas-Recycling-Tag* and *Flaschen*. *Tag* is MSN (masculine, singular, nominative) because it's the subject; therefore the endings are *unser erster*. *Flaschen* is FPA (feminine, plural, accusative) because it is the direct object.

2. Check on the tables to find the correct ending

   The endings, according to the table above, are *keine leeren*.

NOTE: In a classroom or immersion situation, one hears correct German every day. Things "sound right". It's the ideal way to learn. No one goes through an extensive GNC examination every time he or she utters a sentence. Knowing how to determine the GNC of a noun is helpful and should be practiced. It provides a foolproof tool you can rely upon when encountering new constructions throughout the learning experience.

ÜBUNG E **Unser Essen.** On the class trip students ate many different things. Match the adjectives with the foods. Don't forget the GNC for each noun. All these will be accusative because they are direct objects.

EXAMPLE: Rudi hat einen kalten Salat gegessen.

scharf	eine Gurke
kalt	ein Brötchen
süß	ein Apfelsaft
hart	ein Wasser
kalt	ein Salat
sauer	eine Pizza

1. Katja hat _____ gegessen.

2. Hans hat _____ getrunken.

3. Aaron hat _____ gegessen.

4. Adriana hat _____ gegessen.

5. Bettina hat_____ getrunken.

ÜBUNG F **Bildbeschreibung.** Use the pictures to practice writing adjectives. Each picture has two contrasting objects. Write what you see.

EXAMPLE: Ich sehe einen großen Mann und einen kleinen Mann.

1. Ich sehe

   _____

2. _____

3. _____

4. _____

5. _____

| ÜBUNG G | **Eine Email-Beschreibung von Salzburg.** You're enjoying Salzburg. Write an email to your parents describing the city for them. Follow the pattern and use the three adjectives in two different sentences. |

EXAMPLE: der Dom / schön / groß / prachtvoll

      In Salzburg gibt es einen schönen Dom.   Der große Dom ist prachtvoll.

1. der Marktplatz / klein / bunt / interessant

   In Salzburg gibt es _____

2. der Fluss / breit / lang / nicht sehr tief
   NOTE: *sehr* is an adverb modifying *tief*. Adverbs do not take adjective endings.

3. die drei Kirchen / berühmt / klein / wertvoll

   _____

4. das Restaurant / amerikanisch / klein / komisch

   _____

5. die Uni / alt / mittelalterlich / berühmt

   _____

| ÜBUNG H | **Ein Besuch.** You've just heard that your pen pal might be able to visit you this summer. Write a description of your town for him. Include at least six sentence pairs like those in *Übung E*. |

_____

_____

_____

_____

_____

_____

4.   Strong Adjective Endings

Often the adjective stands alone before the noun it modifies.

Kalter Kaffee schmeckt nicht gut.	*Cold coffee doesn't taste good.*
Ich mag alte Schlösser gern.	*I like old castles.*
Wir schlafen in großen Zelten.	*We're sleeping in large tents.*

The following chart shows the strong adjective endings, i.e. the endings you use when the adjective precedes the noun it modifies and there are no *der-* or *ein*-words.

STRONG ADJECTIVE ENDINGS			
	SINGULAR		PLURAL
	MASCULINE	FEMININE	NEUTER	
NOMINATIVE	alt-er	alt-e	alt-es	alt-e
DATIVE	alt-em	alt-er	alt-em	alt-en
ACCUSATIVE	alt-en	alt-e	alt-es	alt-e

ÜBUNG I	**Magst du oder magst du nicht?** In preparation for your upcoming trip to Austria, your pen pal asks you whether you like certain things you may experience in Salzburg. Answer either in the positive or the negative. Vary your answers.

EXAMPLE: die Schlösser / alt   Ich mag alte Schlösser. or Ich mag alte Schlösser nicht.

1. der Fisch / kalt _____

2. der Kaffee / stark _____

3. das Brot / frisch _____

4. die Denkmäler / alt _____

5. die Kirchen / klein _____

Finding the correct adjective ending is much easier than it appears. The table below compares weak, mixed and strong adjective endings in one chart. One part of each expression clearly signals the GNC of the noun, i.e. it looks like the familiar *der-die-das* chart. If there's no *der-die-das* to do so, then the adjective takes those endings.

COMPARISON OF WEAK, STRONG, AND MIXED ADJECTIVE ENDINGS							
	SINGULAR						PLURAL
	MASCULINE		FEMININE		NEUTER		
NOM weak	der	alt-e	die	alt-e	das	alt-e	die	alt-en
mixed	ein	alt-er	eine	alt-e	ein	alt-es	keine	alt-en
strong		alt-er		alt-e		alt-es		alt-e
DAT. weak	dem	alt-en	der	alt-en	dem	alt-en	den	alt-en
mixed	einem	alt-en	einer	alt-en	einem	alt-en	keinen	alt-en
strong		alt-em		alt-er		alt-em		alt-en
ACC. weak	den	alt-en	die	alt-e	das	alt-e	die	alt-en
mixed	einen	alt-en	eine	alt-e	ein	alt-es	keine	alt-en
strong		alt-en		alt-e		alt-es		alt-e

ÜBUNG J	**Ein IM-Gespräch.** You and your friend are talking on Instant Messenger. She tells you what she is bringing on the trip. You reply and tell her that you prefer a different item. React to the list of items.

EXAMPLE: der Pulli / rot /blau   Der rote Pulli ist schön, aber ich finde den blauen Pulli hübsch.

NOTE: In the sentence above it is not necessary to repeat the word *Pulli*. It's clear that the speaker is referring to a blue pullover. The adjective endings (*den blauen*) make it even more evident. They signal that the missing word is MSA. If what's being spoken about is 100% clear to both speaker and listener, than the noun may be eliminated. In such cases, the adjective is then capitalized and becomes the noun.

Der rote Pulli ist schön, aber ich finde den Blauen hübsch.

1. die Bluse / weiß / gelb

_____

2. die Jeans / blau / schwarz

_____

3. die Schuhe / schwarz / braun

_____

4. die Reisetasche / neu / alt

_____

5. der Regenschirm / groß / klein

_____

ÜBUNG K **Siehst du?** Your class is traveling together in a train and you're playing *Siehst du?* One of your classmates will ask if you see what they see. You reply by saying either that you do or don't see it. Vary your answers. When you are done, take a poll in the class to see whether the majority did or didn't see each article.

der Postbus / gelb   Du: Ich sehe einen Postbus.
Dein Partner: Ist es ein gelber Postbus?
Siehst du den gelben Postbus dort drüben?
Du: Ja, genau den Gelben sehe ich.

1. die Wiese / groß _____

_____

_____

2. das Motorrad / knallrot _____

_____

_____

3. das Auto / grün _____

_____

_____

4. der Lastwagen / lang _____

_____

_____

5. das Rathaus / alt _____

_____

_____

| ÜBUNG L | **Der Weg zur Schule.** Choose a point somewhere in your town and write a paragraph about what you see between there and your school. Describe at least five things in order as you see them. Use descriptive adjectives. When you're finished, read your paragraph aloud and ask your classmates to guess where your _Startpunkt_ was. |

_____

_____

_____

_____

_____

_____

_____

| ÜBUNG M | **Der Clown.** While walking to school you had a surprise. You saw a circus clown going into the bank. Another classmate saw one at the gas station. There were clowns all over town. They looked so funny and out of place. On a separate piece of paper, draw a colored picture of yours. Then write a description of him and what he was wearing in as much detail as possible. Tomorrow your classmates will all hang their pictures on the board and read their descriptions. How many clowns can you identify from their descriptions? |

_____

_____

_____

_____

_____

_____

_____

_____

_____

_____

Mein Clown

CHAPTER 7

Present Perfect Tense

1. The Present Perfect Tense

The present perfect tense, often called the conversational past tense, is used to express an action that took place in the past. It is most often formed by using the auxiliary verb *haben* (to have) with the past participle of the verb.

NOTE: A few verbs require the auxiliary verb *sein* (to be). These will be discussed later in this chapter.

The present perfect can be translated in three ways.

Ich habe schwer gearbeitet.
I worked hard. I did work hard. I have worked hard.

Meine Eltern und ich haben Theaterkarten für nächstes Wochenende gekauft.
My parents and I bought/did buy/have bought theater tickets for next weekend.

2. Formation of the Present Perfect Tense

Thinking of the present perfect tense in its third translation (I have seen the film), makes it easier to understand. The verb *haben* (see table below) is used as the finite verb in the sentence. The past participle is added to the end of the sentence or clause without any additional endings.

HABEN	
SINGULAR	PLURAL
ich habe	wir haben
du hast	ihr habt
er, sie, es hat	sie haben
Sie haben	

+ past participle = present perfect tense

Wann hast du dein neues Kleid gekauft?	*When did you buy your new dress?*
Habt ihr schon geklingelt?	*Have you already rung the bell?*
Gestern hat der Lehrer uns in Mathe getestet.	*Yesterday the teacher tested us in Math.*

3.   Formation of the Past Participle in Weak (Regular) Verbs

The past participle of weak verbs is formed by removing the *–en* (or *–n* if there is no *–en*) from the infinitive, then adding a *ge–* before the stem and a *–t* after it.

kaufen	*to buy*	**gekauft**	*bought*
spielen	*to play*	**gespielt**	*played*

ÜBUNG A	**Aufgaben**. Hansi wants to go to a friend's birthday party, but can't go until he assures his mother that he has done all his chores.

EXAMPLE: dein Bett machen   Ja, ich **habe** mein Bett **gemacht**.

1. frühstücken Ja, _____

2. den Hund füttern Ja, _____

3. deine Hausaufgaben machen. Ja, _____

4. Mathe lernen Ja, _____

5. ein Geschenk schon kaufen Ja, _____

ÜBUNG B	**Deine Aufgaben**. Now you want to go to a friend's birthday party. You know your mother will want you to finish certain things before she gives you permission. So you write her a list of what you have already done. Personalize this list to include chores you are expected to do at home.

EXAMPLE: Ich habe mein Bett gemacht.

1. _____

2. _____

3. _____

4. _____

5. _____

a. Verbs with Stems Ending in *-t, -d,* or two Consonants followed by an *-n*

If the stem ends in *-t, -d,* or two consonants followed by an *–n*, a final *–et* is added rather than *–t*. This makes the past participle easier to pronounce.

warten	*wait*	**gewartet**	*waited*	**arbeiten**	*work*	**gearbeitet**	*worked*
öffnen	*open*	**geöffnet**	*opened*	**regnen**	*rain*	**geregnet**	*rained*

ÜBUNG C **Schwesterprobleme.** You're annoyed with your little sister Emilie. It was raining yesterday and she kept you waiting outside ten minutes before opening the door. You're complaining to your mother about the incident.

EXAMPLE: gestern / stark / regnen   Gestern hat es stark geregnet.

1. an die Tür / laut / klopfen

   _____

2. zehn Minuten / warten

   _____

3. endlich / sie / Tür / öffnen

   _____

4. Es war zu spät!   Emilie / meine neue Lederjacke / kaputt / machen

   _____

5. die Jacke / sehr viel / gekostet

   _____

6. ich / wochenlang / für das Geld / arbeiten

   _____

b. Verb with an Inseparable Prefix or Ending in *-ieren*

Do not add the *ge-* if the verb starts with an inseparable prefix *be-, emp-, ent-, er-, ge-, miss-, ver-* or *zer-*, or if the verb ends in *–ieren*.

besuchen	*to visit*	**besucht**	*visited*
erledigen	*to finish*	**erledigt**	*finished*
studieren	*to study*	**studiert**	*studied (at a college or university)*
telefonieren	*to talk on the phone*	**telefoniert**	*talked on the phone*

ÜBUNG D **Versicherungsfoto.** Paul's aunt called and asked him to do her a favor when he was done with his chores. She needed a list of her jewelry for insurance purposes. He took his digital camera and photographed them for her. Relate the day's events.

EXAMPLE: Paul / besuchen / seine Tante Paul hat seine Tante besucht.

1. sie / vorher / mit ihm / telefonieren

   _____

2. er / zuerst / seine Arbeit zu Hause / erledigen

   _____

3. dann / er / bei ihr / ihren Silberschmuck / polieren

   _____

4. die ältere Tante / ihm / die Geschichte von jedem Stück / erzählen

_____

5. er / den Schmuck / fotografieren

_____

6. Paul / ihren Dank / verdienen (earn). So ein netter Neffe!

_____

    c. Verbs with a Separable Prefix

    Verbs with a separable prefix add the _ge-_ between the separable prefix and the
    stem.

anschauen	_to look at_	**angeschaut**	_looked at_
aufräumen	_to clean up_	**aufgeräumt**	_cleaned up_
zuhören	_to listen to_	**zugehört**	_listened to_

ÜBUNG E	**Mutter hat viel gemacht.** Your mother worked very hard yesterday. You are impressed. Tell your father all that your mother accomplished.

EXAMPLE: das Zimmer/aufräumen   Sie **hat** das Zimmer **aufgeräumt.**

1. die Kartoffeln / abputzen

_____

2. die Gläser / auswischen

_____

3. meine Wortschatzsliste (= vocabulary list) / abhören

_____

4. den Hobbyraum/aufräumen

_____

5. eine DVD für heute Abend / abholen

_____

ÜBUNG F	**Das Klassenjournal.** Harald has pictures of everything he did yesterday. Can you help him write about the events for a class journal?

EXAMPLE: Harold hat sein Zimmer aufgeräumt.

1. (abspülen) _____

2. (anschauen) _____

3. (auflegen) _____

4. (wegstellen) _____

5. (zuhören) _____

4.   Formation of the Past Participle of Strong Verbs

The past participle of strong verbs ends in *-en*. The vowel in the verb stem may change in the past participle.

Ich habe einen Apfel gegessen.	*I ate/did eat/ have eaten an apple.*
Habt ihr das Museum leicht gefunden?	*Did you find the museum easily?*
Wann haben wir das Buch gelesen?	*When did we read the book?*

Just as it was necessary to learn the third person present tense of vowel change verbs, e.g., *fahren, er fährt*, it will be necessary to memorize the past participle of strong verbs.

essen, er isst	*eat*	**hat gegessen**	*eaten*
lesen, er liest	*read*	**hat gelesen**	*read*
schlafen, er schläft	*sleep*	**hat geschlafen**	*sleep*
schreiben	*write*	**hat geschrieben**	*written*
sitzen	*sit*	**hat gesessen**	*sat*
sprechen, er spricht	*speak*	**hat gesprochen**	*spoken*
trinken	*drink*	**hat getrunken**	*drunk*

ÜBUNG G	**Stadttag.** While your mother was cleaning, your father spent the day with

your brother in the city. Use the pictures to describe their day.

EXAMPLE: Sie haben einen Film gesehen.

1. _____

2. _____

3. _____

4. _____

5. _____

5.   Formation of the Past Participle of Mixed Verbs

There are a few verbs where the past participles show the vowel change associated with strong verbs, but they end in the -*t* associated with weak verbs. They are called mixed verbs and must also be memorized.

bringen	*to bring*	**gebracht**	*brought*
denken	*to think*	**gedacht**	*thought*
kennen	*to know, be acquainted with*	**gekannt**	*known*
nennen	*to name*	**genannt**	*named*
rennen	*to run*	**gerannt**	*(has) run*
wissen	*to know a fact*	**gewusst**	*known*

There is a complete list of strong and mixed verbs and their principal parts in the appendix on page 200.

ÜBUNG H | **Eine Postkarte an Oma.** In a postcard to your grandmother, you are explaining what your younger brother did yesterday. You write:

EXAMPLE: lange / schlafen   Er hat lange geschlafen.

1. Frühstück / essen

   _____

2. seine Hausaufgaben / zur Schule / bringen

   _____

3. in der Pause / spielen

   _____

4. Freunde / besuchen

   _____

5. einen Film / anschauen

   _____

ÜBUNG I | **Dein Tag.** You're talking to your friend Bettina at lunch. Fill in your half of the conversation. Since you are discussing yesterday's events, use the present perfect tense.

EXAMPLE: Bettina: Was hast du gestern gemacht?
              Du: Ich habe Mathe mit Ernst gelernt. Und du?

1. **BETTINA:** Ich habe den neuen King Kong Film gesehen.

   DU: _____

2. **BETTINA:** Ja, ich habe ihn sehr gut gefunden. Habt ihr den ganzen Nachmittag gelernt?

   DU: _____

3. **BETTINA:** Wer hat gewonnen? Normalerweise ist Ernst ein guter Spieler.

   DU: _____

4. **BETTINA:** Habt ihr etwas gegessen?

   DU: _____

5. BETTINA: Selbstgebacken? Oder hast du sie gekauft?

   DU: _____

6.   Present Participle Using *sein*

SEIN	
SINGULAR	PLURAL
ich **bin**	wir **sind**
du **bist**	ihr **seid**
er, sie, es **ist**	sie **sind**
Sie **sind**	

+ past participle = present perfect tense

NOTE: The present perfect tense uses *haben* as an auxiliary verb. There are exceptions however. Verbs which indicate motion from one place to another (walk, run, go), a state of being (am, are, is) or change in a state of being (become, be born, die) are called intransitive verbs, and do not take an object. These verbs use the auxiliary verb *sein* instead of *haben* in the present perfect tense.

Wir sind nach Duisburg gefahren.	*We drove to Duisburg.*
Wann bist du angekommen?	*When did you arrive?*
Ich bin am Samstag ins Kino gegangen.	*I went to the movies on Saturday.*
Goethe ist im Jahre 1832 gestorben.	*Goethe died in the year 1832.*

Some of the most common verbs that use *sein* are:

abfahren	*depart*	**ist abgefahren**	*departed*
ankommen	*arrive*	**ist angekommen**	*arrived*
fahren	*drive, ride*	**ist gefahren**	*drove, rode*
gehen	*go*	**ist gegangen**	*gone*
kommen	*come*	**ist gekommen**	*come*
laufen	*run, walk*	**ist gelaufen**	*walked, run*
schwimmen	*swim*	**ist geschwommen**	*swum*
sein	*be*	**ist gewesen**	*been*
sterben	*die*	**ist gestorben**	*died*

ÜBUNG J   **Mein idealer Ferientag.** You want to give your pen pal an impression of what you like and don't like. You've decided to describe one of the best vacation days you've enjoyed in the past.

EXAMPLE: aufstehen / erst / um elf /   Ich bin erst um elf aufgestanden.

1. gehen / langsam / in die Küche

   _____

2. dann / zwei Stunden / in der Küche / sein

   _____

3. gegen Mittag / in dem Park / ankommen

   _____

4. zur Schwimmhalle / laufen

   _____

5. dann / nach Hause / zurückgehen

   _____

6. später / mit dem Rad / fahren

   _____

ÜBUNG K   **Ein normaler Tag.** Unfortunately not all days are vacation days. Write a paragraph about any day last week. Mention at least six things that you did.

_____

_____

_____

_____

_____

_____

ÜBUNG L   **Email an die Eltern.** Josh has just arrived to spend a month in Austria with a host family. He sends the following e-mail to his parents. Complete his message with the appropriate forms of the verb and auxiliary verb as indicated.

Hallo liebe Eltern!

Ich ___bin___ gut ___angekommen___ . Die Mutter _____ mich um zehn Uhr am Flughafen
                              ankommen

_____ . Ich _____ meine neue Familie _____ und _____ mein neues
     abholen   kennenlernen

Zimmer _____. Alles gefällt mir sehr gut. Die Familie _____ mir am Nachmittag ihre
          sehen

Stadt _____. Toll! Ich finde alles super. Um sieben Uhr _____ wir zu Abend
        zeigen

_____. Dann _____ ich euch schnell diese Email _____ und _____
  essen   schreiben

sofort ins Bett _____.
              gehen

Bis später!

Josh

ÜBUNG M **Jakob**. Create a story about a fictional character called "Jakob." Use the
following sentence elements to create a journal entry about what he did
yesterday.

EXAMPLE: Jakob ist in die Stadt gegangen.

in die Stadt	gehen
die Hauptstrasse entlang	spazieren
ein Eis	essen
Maja und Katja	sehen
mit ihnen	sprechen
ein Buch	kaufen

_____

_____

_____

_____

_____

_____

| ÜBUNG N | **Der Lotteriegewinntag.** You won the lottery! You went places, bought things and did things with no thought about what they cost. It was a glorious day! Write your pen pal and tell her everything you did, or at least eight things in a well-written, interesting letter. Remember to vary your word order to add interest. |

_____

_____

_____

_____

_____

_____

_____

_____

_____

_____

CHAPTER 8
Reflexive Pronouns and Verbs

1. What is a Reflexive Pronoun?

In German, an object pronoun can be the direct object, the indirect object, or the object of a preposition. Sometimes an object pronoun in a sentence is the same person or thing as the subject.

Der Hund kratzt sich. *The dog (subject) is scratching himself.*
Der Hund kratzt ihn. *The dog (subject) is scratching him.*

In the first sentence above, the dog and himself are the same animal.
In the second sentence, the dog and him are two different beings.

The first sentence is reflexive. The object pronoun "reflects" the subject, i.e. it is the same as the subject. English adds the word "self" or "selves" to the pronoun to signal that the person or persons are the same as the subject. German uses the reflexive pronoun.

ÜBUNG A **Ein bisschen englische Grammatik.** Before learning the German, your teacher has asked that you review the concept in English. Which of the two sentences in the sentence pairs is reflexive? Circle the letter. Indicate how many people are being discussed in each sentence.

EXAMPLE: (A) My daughter is feeding herself for the first time. _____ one _____

(B) My daughter is feeding her for the first time. _____ two _____

1. A. She's pinching her to keep her awake. _____

   B. She's pinching herself to stay awake. _____

2. A. They're treating them to dinner tonight. _____

   B. They're treating themselves to dinner tonight. _____

3. A. The lawyer is defending himself in court today. _____

   B. The lawyer is defending him in court today. _____

2. The Reflexive Pronoun

REFLEXIVE PRONOUNS					
NOMINATIVE PRONOUN		DATIVE REFLEXIVE PRONOUN		PRONOUN ACCUSATIVE REFLEXIVE	
ich	I	mir	(to or for) myself	mich	myself
du	you (informal)	dir	(to or for) yourself	dich	yourself
er, sie, es	he, sie it	sich	(to or for) himself, herself, itself	sich	himself, herself, itself
wir	we	uns	(to or for) ourselves	uns	ourselves
ihr	you (plural)	euch	(to or for) yourselves	euch	yourselves
sie	they	sich	(to or for) themselves	sich	themselves
Sie	you (formal)	sich	(to or for) yourself/yourselves	sich	yourself, yourselves

ÜBUNG B **Wie viele Leute?** How many people are involved in these sentences?

EXAMPLE: Die Frau hat sich in Marbach ein Buch gekauft. ___1___

1. Hans hat sich eine Kamera für die Reise gekauft. _____

2. Herr Marzipan hat sich einen neuen Stadtplan gekauft. _____

3. Maria hat ihr ein Buch von Marbach mitgebracht. _____

4. Melanie wäscht sie. _____

5. Was hast du dir gekauft? _____

ÜBUNG C **Ein Missverständnis.** Many of the students on the trip think that some people did things for other people. That is a misunderstanding. You know that they really did things for themselves. Correct the statements.

EXAMPLE: Herr Marzipan hat ihm einen neuen Stadtplan gekauft.
          Nein, er hat sich einen neuen Stadtplan gekauft.

1. Frau Ganz hat ihr eine CD von der Stadtkappelle mitgebracht.

   Nein, sie _____

2. Margot hat uns einen neuen Museumsführer gekauft.

   Nein, sie _____

3. Niels und Niela haben uns Konzertkarten gekauft.

   Nein, sie _____

4. Danielle hat mir eine Museumseintrittskarte mitgebracht.

   Nein, sie _____

5. Ich habe Maria eine Schilleruhr gekauft.

   Nein, du _____

| ÜBUNG D | **Haben Sie sich das gekauft? Herr Marzipan kauft ein.** Herr Marzipan bought a number of interesting things. You want to know for whom he bought these things. You ask him if he bought them for himself and he answers. |

EXAMPLE: Haben Sie sich das Schillerbuch gekauft?   Ja   Ja, ich habe es mir gekauft.
           Haben Sie sich die CD's gekauft? Nein (er)   Nein, ich habe sie ihm gekauft.

1. Haben Sie sich die Theaterkarten gekauft?   Ja

   _____

2. Haben Sie sich eine Schilleruhr gekauft?   Nein (meine Mutter)

   _____

3. Haben Sie sich einen neuen Stadtplan gekauft?   Ja

   _____

4. Haben Sie sich auch einen blauen Mantel gekauft?   Nein (mein Sohn)

   _____

3.   Reflexive Verbs

Certain verbs in German require that the subject be mentioned twice in a sentence: once as the subject and then again as one of the objects in the sentence. These are called reflexive verbs and are used far more frequently in German than in English.

Ich wasche mich.	*I am washing (myself).*
Sie zieht sich an.	*She is dressing (herself).*
Wir setzen uns hin.	*We are sitting (ourselves) down.*
Putzt euch die Zähne, Kinder!	*Brush your teeth, children*
	(Literally, clean to yourselves the teeth, children.)

On the next page is a list of common reflexive verbs. In the case of strong and/or stem change verbs, the third person singular present tense and past participles are included.

sich anziehen, hat angezogen	*dress (oneself)*
sich baden	*take a bath*
sich beeilen	*hurry, rush (oneself)*
sich benehmen, benimmt, hat benommen	*behave (oneself)*
sich kämmen	*comb one's hair*
sich duschen	*shower*
sich erkälten	*catch a cold*
sich irren	*err, make a mistake*
sich rasieren	*shave*
sich schämen	*be ashamed*
sich (hin)setzen	*sit down*
sich vorstellen	*introduce oneself*
sich schminken	*put on makeup*

ÜBUNG E | **Muttersworte!** Marco's and Maria's mother reminds them what to do every morning. Write the commands she might give.

EXAMPLE: sich benehmen   Benehmt euch!

1. sich anziehen _____

2. sich duschen _____

3. sich beeilen _____

4. sich hinsetzen _____

ÜBUNG F | **Deine Morgenroutine.** Write your pen pal a message telling him what you do each morning before school.

EXAMPLE: morgens / sich baden   Morgens bade ich mich.

1. sich rasieren _____

2. sich anziehen _____

3. sich kämmen _____

4. zum Frühstück / sich hinsetzen _____

5. sich beeilen _____

6. sich schminken _____

4.   Dative Reflexive Pronouns with Parts of the Body

Often where English uses the possessive adjective German uses a reflexive pronoun.

Hast du dir das Bein gebrochen?	*Did you break your leg?*
	(literally) Did you break to yourself the leg?
Er putzt sich die Zähne.	*He's brushing his teeth.*
	(literally) He's cleaning to himself the teeth.
Wir waschen uns die Hände.	*We are washing our hands.*
	(literally) We're washing to ourselves the hands.

Since the body part mentioned is the direct object, the reflexive becomes the indirect object and is therefore in the dative case.

> **ÜBUNG G**   **Morgenroutine.** Write down what others in your family do regularly in the morning.

EXAMPLE: Meine Schwester rasiert sich die Beine.

1. Mein Bruder _____

2. Meine Schwester _____

3. Meine Mutter _____

4. Ich _____

ÜBUNG H   **Carlas Morgenroutine.** Carla needs help writing a story about her mornings. Combine the sentence elements for her. Not all are reflexive sentences.

EXAMPLE: Carla / jeden Tag / sich duschen   Carla duscht sich jeden Tag.

1. Carla / um sechs Uhr / aufstehen

_____

2. Sie / das Gesicht / immer / sich waschen

_____

3. Dann / sich anziehen / und / kämmen

_____

4. Danach / sie / sich schminken

_____

5. fast jeden Tag / sie / ihre Jeans / sich anziehen

_____

6. sie / die Zähne / sich putzen

_____

ÜBUNG I   **Videogeschichte.** Write out this story board for a video you are making about you daily routine.

EXAMPLE: Ich putze mir die Zähne.

1. _____

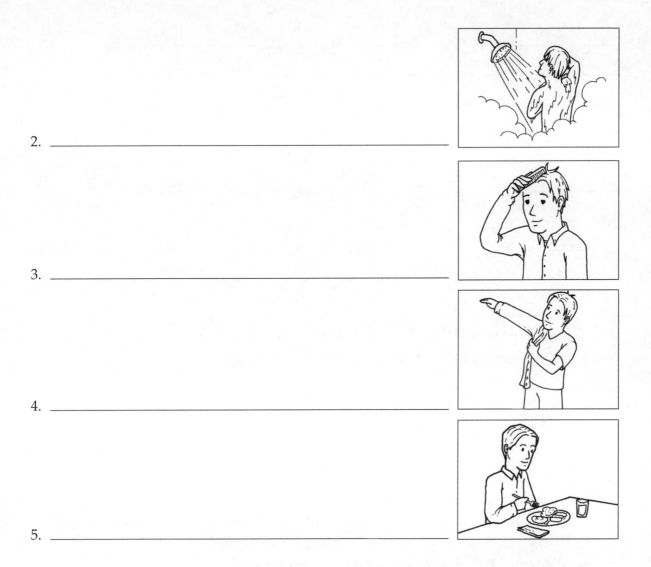

2. _____

3. _____

4. _____

5. _____

| ÜBUNG J | **Tagesablauf.** Use the verbs to write an e-mail describing what you do each day. You must add some time adverbs: *dann, danach, um sieben Uhr, zuerst,* etc. |

sich anziehen, hat sich angezogen	*dress (oneself)*
sich ausziehen, hat sich ausgezogen	*undress (oneself)*
aufstehen	*get up*
sich baden	*take a bath*
sich beeilen	*hurry, rush (oneself)*
sich die Haare bürsten / kämmen	*brush / comb one's hair*
sich duschen	*shower*
Frühstuck essen	*eat breakfast*
sich die Zähne putzen	*brush one's teeth*
sich rasieren	*shave*
sich schminken	*put on makeup*

_____

_____

_____

_____

_____

_____

_____

_____

5.   Accusative Reflexive Pronouns with Emotions

The reflexive is often used in German to express emotions.

sich ärgern	*get angry*
sich blamieren	*be embarassed*
sich freuen	*be happy, rejoice*
sich schämen	*be ashamed*

Der Professor ärgert sich, dass seine ganze Klasse unvorbereitet ist.

The professor is angry that his entire class is unprepared.

Die Studenten in der Klasse schämen sich, dass sie unvorbereitet sind.

The students in the class are ashamed that they are unprepared.

Alle freuen sich, dass es schon Freitag Nachmittag ist.

Everyone is happy that it's already Friday afternoon.

| ÜBUNG K | **Er schämt sich.** How do you think the people felt about what happened?

EXAMPLE: Norbert hat eine schlechte Note in Mathe bekommen.
          Er schämt sich, dass er eine schlechte Note bekommen hat.

1. Natalie hat das Spiel gewonnen.

_____

2. Alfons hat das Spiel verloren.

_____

3. Er weiss nicht warum.

_____

4. Er ist wütend geworden

_____

6.   Reflexive Verbs with Preposition Completers

Often a verb needs a prepositional phrase to complete its meaning: "She's applying for a job." To "apply for" is a combination that belongs together. There are also verb-preposition combinations that are always used together in German. Some of the more common reflexive verb-preposition combinations are listed below. (NOTE: For a more complete list of verb-prepositions combinations, refer to chapter 18.)

sich ärgern über + accusative	*be angry about*
sich beschäftigen mit + dative	*be occupied with*
sich freuen auf + accusative	*look forward to*
sich freuen über + accusative	*be happy about*
sich interessieren für + accusative	*be interested in*

ÜBUNG L   **Eine Umfrage.** You've asked your classmates about their interests and now need to record the results for the Klassenbuch.

EXAMPLE: Marta / Schach / sich interessieren für
Marta interessiert sich für Schach.

1. Bob / Fussball / nicht / sich interessieren für

_____

2. Debora / Basketball / sich beschäftigen mit

_____

3. Anna / ein gutes Handballspiel / sich freuen auf

_____

4. Anika / nicht / der neue Harry Potter Film / sich interessieren für

_____

5. Viktor / viel / der neue Roman von Cornelia Funke / sich freuen auf

_____

ÜBUNG M   **Mich ärgert's.** Make a list of things that make you angry.

EXAMPLE: Ich ärgere mich über dumme Leute.

1. _____

2. _____

3. _____

4. _____

5. _____

ÜBUNG N   **Ich freue mich auf . . .** Because of the recent trip to Salzburg, you've watched
the film "The Sound of Music" again. In it, the von Trapp children sang about
their "Favorite Things." With a partner or on your own, create your a song or
poem about things you enjoy. Use any of the reflexives in this chapter to
express yourself.

Ich freue mich auf die schönen Blumen.

_____

_____

_____

_____

_____

_____

_____

_____

CHAPTER 9
Dative Verbs andAdjectives

1. Dative Verbs

Certain verbs in German require a dative object rather than the customary accusative object. A list of the most common dative verbs follows.

ähneln	*resemble*	**glauben**	*believe (s.o.)*
antworten	*answer*	**gratulieren**	*congratulate*
befehlen, befiehlt	*command*	**helfen, hilft**	*help*
hat befohlen		**hat geholfen**	
danken	*thank*	**Leid tun, tut Leid**	*be sorry*
dienen	*serve*	**hat Leid getan**	
einfallen fällt ein,	*occur to*	**mislingen, ist mislungen**	*fail*
ist eingefallen		**passen**	*fit*
erlauben	*allow*	**passieren, ist passiert**	*happen*
fehlen	*be missing*	**schaden**	*harm*
folgen	*follow*	**verzeihen, hat verziehen**	*pardon,*
gefallen, gefällt	*please, to be*		*forgive*
hat gefallen	*pleasing to*	**wehtun, tut weh,**	*hurt*
gehorchen	*obey*	**hat weh getan**	
gehören	*belong to*	**zuhören (sep. prefix)**	*listen to*
gelingen, ist gelungen	*be successful*		

Mir hat Marbach gefallen.	*I liked Marbach.*
Wir danken dem Lehrer für den Ausflug.	*We thank the teacher for the trip.*
Gehorchst du immer deinen Eltern?	*Do you always obey your parents?*

For a review of the dative endings and pronouns, see chapter 4.

ÜBUNG A **Mir gefällt das**. Tell whether your friends and you liked or didn't like (*gefallen*) the following things you might see during a typical city tour. You must use pronouns to sound really German.

EXAMPLE: (Hans) Ihm hat das alte Rathaus gefallen.
Ihm hat das alte Rathause nicht gefallen.

1. (du) _____

2. (Margot) _____

3. (Hans und Margot) _____

4. (Frau Mahrens) _____

5. (Michael) _____

| ÜBUNG B | **Ein Durcheinander.** You've been on a class trip and are now back on the bus.

EXAMPLE: du, Johanna / die blaue Tasche / gehören?
Johanna, gehört dir die blaue Tasche?

1. Sie, Herr Marzipan / der große Stadtplan / gehören?

_____

2. ihr, Margot und Marlies / die neuen Stadtführer / gehören?

_____

3. du, Sebastian / der Museumsführer / gehören?

   _____

4. du, Ralf / ein blauer Pulli / fehlen?

   _____

5. Sie, Frau Mahrens / die Stadtkapelle CDs / fehlen?

   _____

ÜBUNG C	**Ein Sprachdurcheinander.** Everyone is talking so loudly on the ride back from your outing. You have to mentally fill in a few blanks to understand what everyone was saying.

EXAMPLE: Jan: Johanna, was hat __dir__ am besten in Marbach gefallen?

1. JOHANNA: Das Schiller Museum hat _____ gut gefallen.
2. JAN: Ich glaube _____ Johanna! Du warst eine Stunde darin.
3. JOHANNA: Aber Jan, du bist _____ ins Museum gefolgt.
4. PETER: Johanna, er folgt _____ immer.
5. JAN: Freut _____ nicht! Was weiß er?
6. PETER: Ich danke _____, Astrid, für die Idee. Das Museum war sehr interessant.
7. HANNA: Oh ja, die Geschichte hat _____ auch gefallen.
8. SANDRA: _____ fällt es jetzt ein, dass Schiller auch „Die Räuber" geschrieben hat.
9. HANNA: Echt? Das Drama hat _____ immer gut gefallen.
10. PETER: _____ fehlt meine Jacke. Hat jemand sie gesehen?

ÜBUNG D	**Marbach gefällt mir.** One conversation catches your attention, but you still have problems hearing. Combine the sentence elements which you hear Margot say.

EXAMPLE: Marbach / nicht / gefallen   Mir hat Marbach nicht gefallen.

1. es / einfallen / dass / der Mathematiker Tobias Mayer / auch / in Marburg / leben

   _____

2. ihr / glauben (imperative)

   _____!

3. Die neugotische Alexanderkirche / die Harmonie / von der Altstadt / schaden

   _____

4. Moment mal / der Stadtplan / ich / fehlen. Wo ist er?

   _____

5. du / antworten (imperative)

   _____

6. ich / du / nicht / antworten

_____

| ÜBUNG E | **Raucher oder Nichtraucher.** On the bus you hear two students arguing. Use the sentence elements to write down what they were saying.

EXAMPLE: ich / nicht / du / Joseph / verzeihen / können
Ich kann dir nicht verzeihen, Joseph!

1. Rauchen / die Gesundheit / schaden

_____

2. ja / das / ich / du / glauben

_____

3. aber / du /ich /zuhören / sollen

_____

4. aber / meine / Mutter / ich / es / erlauben

_____

5. das / ich / Leid tun. Rauchen / ich / nicht / gefallen

_____

Janna and Peter are at a standoff. He wants to smoke and she doesn't want him to.
Using at least 3 dative verbs, finish off their conversation. It's up to you whether they finish
up the trip friends or are still quarreling over this issue.

_____

_____

_____

_____

_____

_____

2.   Dative Adjectives

Some adjectives are combined with a dative noun. Another way to say "I don't know
that" is to say "That is not known to me." _Das ist mir nicht bekannt._ While unfamiliar
in English, it is a common construction in German. Also frequently used in German is
the combination of the following adjectives with a dative object.

ähnlich	_similar_	**hilfreich**	_helpful_
bekannt	_known_	**lästig**	_bothersome_

böse	angry, evil		
fremd	foreign, strange	nützlich	useful
gehorsam	obedient	peinlich	embarassing
gleich	same, similar	schädlich	harmful
(un)möglich	(im) possible		

Der Lehrer ist seinen Schülern böse.	*The teacher is angry at his students.*
Dein Benehmen ist mir echt peinlich.	*Your behavior is genuinely embarrassing to me.*
Das ist ihm gleich.	*He doesn't care. (literally; it's the same to him.)*

NOTE: A popular German slang expression, used only in situations where casual language is appropriate, is *Das ist mir Wurst* (or *egal*). Even stronger and somewhat argumentative is *Das ist mir völlig Wurst* (or *egal*). The translation is "I don't care," or the stronger "I couldn't care less."

ÜBUNG F   **Umfrage nach dem Ausflug.** You interview students and teachers after the trip. While most enjoyed it, you happen to choose the few who weren't so enthusiastic. Use a dative adjective construction to create their answers.

EXAMPLE: Ralf, möchtest du über das Museum oder über die Kirche berichten?   gleich
Das ist mir gleich.

1. Johanna, wie hast du die Stadttour gefunden?   zu lang und lästig

_____

2. Herr Marzipan, wie war das Benehmen von den Schülern?   peinlich

_____

3. Ralf, wie waren die Beschreibungen von den Sehenswürdigkeiten?   nicht nützlich

_____

4. Frau Mahrens, wie waren die Schüler?   nicht gehorsam

_____

5. Marika und Meiko, wie war die Hinfahrt?   zu lang

_____

ÜBUNG G   **Positives über Marbach.** During the interview, one student found everything to have been a positive experience. Match the columns to write what Petra said.

EXAMPLE: Mir war die Kirche nicht bekannt.

die Kirche	sehr nützlich
die Stadttour	nicht peinlich
das Benehmen von den Schülern	hilfreich
der Museumsführer	nicht lästig
die Museumstour	nicht bekannt

1. _____

2. _____

3. _____

4. _____

| ÜBUNG H | **Das Interview**. You are preparing interview questions for your classmates. Using at least four dative verbs and two dative adjectives write down your questions so that you are ready for the interview. |

EXAMPLE: Was war für dich auf der Reise ärgerlich?
Ist dir etwas mislungen?

_____

_____

_____

_____

_____

_____

_____

_____

_____

CHAPTER 10
Comparatives

1. The Comparative of Adjectives and Adverbs

An adjective modifies a noun. The correct ending for adjectives is determined by identifying the GNC (gender, number and case) of the noun they modify. (For a review of adjective endings refer back to chapter 6.)

FSN   FSN
Meine Mutter ist fantastisch! She ist eine gute Köchin.

My mother is fantastic! She's a good cook.

Adverbs, words which modify an adjective, verb or another adverb, are even easier to use. They never take endings. Adverbs answer the questions "how," "when," "where," and "to what extent."

Meine Tante kocht fantastisch. Wir essen oft und gerne bei ihr.
Gut kann sie kochen.

My aunt cooks fantastically. We eat at her home often and enjoy it.
She can cook well.

2. Comparing Two Persons or Things Using the Positive

Adjectives and adverbs have three forms: the positive (good), the comparative (better), and the superlative (best). The easiest way to compare two equal things is to follow this simple pattern in German.

(genau) so . . . wie	*(just/exactly) as . . . as*
Er ist **(genau)** so alt **wie** ich.	*He is (just/exactly) as old as I.*

NOTE: The noun or pronoun directly following *wie* will be in the nominative case.

Mein Bruder ist genau so groß wie ich.

My brother is just as tall as I (am).

ÜBUNG A | **So gut wie . . .** You hear two children talking about their families. Each is claiming that his family is just as good as the other's. Fill in the missing parts of the conversation.

EXAMPLE: MIKA – Mein Vater ist sehr intelligent.
TIM – Mein Vater ist genau so intelligent wie dein Vater.

1. MIKA – Meine Mutter kocht sehr gut!

   TIM _____

2. MIKA – Mein Bruder kriegt ausgezeichnete Noten in der Schule.

   TIM _____

3. MIKA – Unser Auto ist sehr schon.

   TIM _____

4. MIKA – Meine Schwester spielt fantastisch Fussball.

   TIM _____

5. Mein Haus ist sehr groß.

   TIM _____

NOTE: Adding *nicht* (not) or *nicht ganz* (not quite) creates comparisons of unequal persons or things.

nicht so . . . . **wie**	*not as . . . . as*
Sie ist **nicht so** nett **wie** ich.	*She is **not as** nice **as I**.*
nicht ganz so . . . . **wie**	*not quite as . . . as*
Er spielt Tennis **nicht ganz** so gut **wie** ich.	*He doesn't play tennis **quite as** well as I (do).*

ÜBUNG B **Doch nicht so gut wie . . .** Mika replies that Tim's statements are not true. Use the statements from *Übung A*.

EXAMPLE: Dein Vater ist nicht (ganz) so intelligent wie mein Vater.

1. _____
2. _____
3. _____
4. _____
5. _____

ÜBUNG C **Ein Buchbericht.** Your friend is on the phone and you can only hear one side of the conversation.

EXAMPLE: Cornelia Funke / JK Rowling / gut / schreiben
Cornelia Funke schreibt genau so gut wie JK Rowling.

1. Scipio / Harry Potter / interessant / sein 👎

_____

2. Venedig / Hogwarts / bezaubernd / sein 👍

_____

3. die Geschichte von Harry / die Geschichte von Scipio / aufregend / sein 👍

_____

4. Harrys Freunde / Bos Freunde / treu / sein 👎

_____

5. Rowling / Funke / viele Bücher / schreiben (present perfect) 👎

_____

ÜBUNG D **Cornelia Funke, Autorin.** You are reading a review in your school newspaper about Cornelia Funke. She writes books in Germany that are often compared favorably to J. K. Rowling's Harry Potter books. Unfortunately, you have dripped some of your drink on the review and have to supply a few missing words.

Die englischen Harry Potter Bücher sind _____ Cornelia Funkes. Harry
just as good as

Potter ist _____ Funkes Charakter Scipio in „Herr der Diebe". Ihr
just as interesting as

nächstes Buch „Tintenherz" ist aber _____ „Herr der Diebe". Ich habe es
not quite as good as

_____ „Harry Potter und der Gefangene von Askaban" gelesen. Beide
not as gladly as

Autoren sind aber lesenswert.

ÜBUNG E **Sind meine so gut wie deine?** How do your things stack up? Are they as good or not as good as your friends'? Interview a fellow student in German and then decide how your grades, house, etc. compare to his or hers.

EXAMPLE: mein Auto   Mein Auto ist genau so groß wie Marias.
or Mein Auto is nicht ganz so groß wit Marias.

1. meine Noten

_____

2. mein Fahrrad

_____

3. mein Freund / meine Freundin

_____

4. mein Haus

_____

5. meine Stereoanlage

_____

3. Formation of the Comparative

The formation of the comparative in English is complex. It is formed by adding –er to adjectives and adverbs of one syllable: older, wiser, richer, and poorer. If the adjective has two syllables and ends in –y, English changes the y to an i and then adds –er: "wealthier," "happier," "and "easier." If the adjectives or adverbs have more than one syllable and do not end in –y, English uses the word "more" plus the adjective: "more beautiful," "more intelligent."

In German, the formation of the comparative is much easier. All adjectives and adverbs add an –er regardless of how many syllables: _intelligenter, langsamer, schneller, reicher, interessanter._ If the adjective only has one syllable that includes an _a, o,_ or _u_ (not _au_), then it will probably take an _umlaut_ in the comparative. There are only a few exceptions, which include:

toll, toller	_great, greater; amazing, more amazing_
schlank, schlanker	_slender, more slender_
nass, nasser	_wet, wetter_

NOTE: Below is a list of the most common adjectives that take an _umlaut_ in the comparative.

alt, älter	_old, older_
arm, ärmer	_poor, poorer_
dumm, dümmer	_dumb, dumber_
gesund, gesünder	_healthy, healthier_
groß, grösser	_big, bigger; tall, taller_
jung, jünger	_young, younger_
kalt, kälter	_cold, colder_
krank, kränker	_sick, sicker_
klug, klüger	_clever, more clever_
lang, länger	_long, longer_
schwach, schwächer	_weak, weaker_
stark, stärker	_strong, stronger_
warm, wärmer	_warm, warmer_

ÜBUNG F	**Charaktervergleich.** You overhear a discussion between two students about the characters in Cornelia Funke's and JK Rowling's books. Write out the objections that the second person utters.

EXAMPLE: Prosper und Bo sind intelligent. Aber Harry ist intelligenter!

1. Harrys Leben ist interessant. Aber Bos leben ist _____.

2. Venedig ist schön. Aber Hogwarts ist _____.

3. Das Leben von Harry ist schwer. Aber Bo und Prosperos Leben ist _____.

4. Harrys Tante ist streng. Aber Bos Tante ist _____.

5. Harrys Freunde sind klug. Aber Prosperos Freunde sind _____.

6. Harry ist jung. Aber Bo ist _____.

7. Scipio ist toll. Aber Dumbledore ist _____.

8. Fudge ist dumm. Aber der Detektiv ist _____.

9. Das Karussell ist alt. Aber Hogwarts ist _____.

10. Harry Potter Bücher sind abenteuerlich. Aber Funke Bücher sind _____.

4.   Using Comparative Adjectives

When modifying a noun, comparative adjectives take the same endings as their positive form. (See chapter 6.) They match the GNC of the noun it modifies.

Eine interessantere Schule als Hogwarts findest du nie.
FSA – DO

You'll never find a more interesting school than Hogwarts.

Mein älterer Bruder heißt Paul. Mein jüngerer Bruder heißt Sven.

My older brother is called Paul. My younger brother is called Sven.

ÜBUNG G   **Eine Buchbesprechung.** You are reading an online critique of the Harry Potter books. Some of the remarks are not clear. Fill in the blanks.

EXAMPLE: Einen interessant**eren** Roman findest du nie.

1. Die älter_____ Weasley Brüder erscheinen nicht in diesem Buch.

2. Eine nett_____ Frau als Frau Weasley kommt selten in Literatur vor.

3. Von einem klüg_____ Magier als Dumbledore habe ich nie gelesen.

4. Der jüng_____ Weasley Bruder heißt Ron.

5. Im Vergleich mit Draco ist Harry der stärk_____ Junge.

5. Comparing Two Unequal Persons or Things Using the Comparative

In German, the comparative form of the adjective and the word *als* is used to compare two unequal persons or things.

J.K. Rowlings letztes Harry Potter Buch ist länger als ihr erstes Buch.

J.K. Rowling's last Harry Potter book is longer than her first book.

Harry Potter ist älter als ich und jünger als mein Freund.

Harry Potter is older than I and younger than my friend.

a. Negative comparisons can be formed by adding *nicht*.

Ginny ist **nicht** größer als ihr Bruder.

*Ginny is **not** taller than her brother.*

ÜBUNG H │ **Literatengespräch.** Your friends, both literature fans, are having a discussion. Use the sentence elements to express what Jon says.

EXAMPLE: JANNA – „Der Herr Der Diebe" ist interessant.
JON – Ja, aber Harry Potter ist <u>interessanter</u> als „Der Herr Der Diebe".

1. JANNA – Harry ist sehr jung.

   JON – Das ist wahr, aber Bo ist _____ als Harry.

2. JANNA – Hogwarts ist verzaubert.

   JON – Ja, aber Venedig ist doch _____ als Hogwarts.

3. JANNA – Das stimmt, Venedig ist eine schöne Stadt.

   JON – Ach ja, London ist doch nicht _____ als Venedig.

4. JANNA – Ich glaube, dass die Schildkröte sehr süß ist.

   JON – Das ist sie, aber nicht _____ als die Tiere von Hagrid.

5. JANNA – Das ist wahr, aber die Schildkröte ist intelligent.

   JON – Ja, aber nicht _____ als der Drachen.

ÜBUNG I │ **Charaktervergleich.** For a survey in your class you are asked to compare at least five different characters from books you have read or movies you have seen.

EXAMPLE: Ich finde Harry Potters Freundin Hermione viel intelligenter als Susan aus dem Buch „Narnia".

1. _____

2. _____

3. _____

4. _____

5. _____

b. Adverbs follow the same rule.

Bodo singt lauter aber nicht besser als sein Bruder Bernd.
Bodo sings louder but not better than his brother Bernd.

| ÜBUNG J | **Wer tut was besser?** (Who does what better?) When you're done, compare your answers with those of your classmates. Did they think in general that the characters from JK Rowling's books were better/faster/more intelligent than those in Cornelia Funke's books, or vice versa? |

EXAMPLE: Harry / Draco / schnell / fliegen   Harry fliegt schneller als Draco.

1. Hermione / Ginny / laut / singen
   _____

2. Hagrid / Mr. Fudge / komisch / aussehen
   _____

3. ein Quidditchspiel / ein Fußballspiel / lang / dauern
   _____

4. Fußballspieler / Quidditchspieler / hart / spielen
   _____

5. Viktor Krumm / Cedric Diggory / fair / spielen
   _____

| ÜBUNG K | **Selbstbeschreibung.** Compare yourself and how you do things to people you know and to fictional characters. Use your imagination. Truth is not important here. |

EXAMPLE: Ich singe besser als Elvis Presley.
        Ich bin intelligenter als Artemis Fowl.

1. _____
2. _____
3. _____
4. _____
5. _____

6. Irregular Comparatives

There are only six adjectives and adverbs that change in the comparative. This list will have to be memorized.

COMPARATIVE OF IRREGULAR ADJECTIVES AND ADVERBS			
POSITIVE		**COMPARATIVE**	
bald	*soon*	**eher**	*sooner*
gern	*gladly*	**lieber**	*preferably, more gladly*
gut	*good*	**besser**	*better*
groß	*large, tall, big*	**größer**	*larger, taller, bigger*
hoch	*high*	**höher**	*higher*
viel	*much, many*	**mehr**	*more*

ÜBUNG L   **Fantasiebücher.** Your class is doing a comparison of popular fantasy books. You're transcribing your notes for the class book. Fill in the blanks to complete your entry.

EXAMPLE: Kriminalromane sind gut, aber fantastische Geschichten sind _besser_ .

1. Rowling hat viele Bücher geschrieben. Funke hat aber_____ geschrieben. (**NOTE:** Rowling hat bis 2006 Bücher 5 veröffentlicht, Funke mehr als 30.)

2. Mario liest Rowling gern, aber er hat Funke _____.

3. „Narnia" ist sehr gut, aber Ana findet „Harry Potter" _____.

4. Hogwarts ist auf einem Berg. Es liegt viel _____ als Venedig.

5. Venedig ist groß, aber London ist eine viel _____ Stadt.

ÜBUNG M   **Eine Umfrage.** Make a survey among your friends to see who does things better, faster, slower, more often, etc. than others. You may also compare appearance and personality. Your comments must be courteous.

EXAMPLE: Ulla spielt Basketball besser als Julio.
Martin ist kleiner als Martina.

1. _____

2. _____

3. _____

4. _____

5. _____

CHAPTER 11
Conjunctions
Subordinate Clauses

1.   Coordinating Conjunctions

Coordinating conjunctions combine two independent clauses. An independent clause is one that can stand alone as a sentence.

Wir zelten nächstes Wochenende am Tegernsee, aber meine Freundin kann leider nicht mitkommen.

We're camping next weekend at the Tegernsee, but unfortunately my girlfriend can't come along.

In the sentence above, the clauses are connected by the coordinating conjunction *aber*. Both clauses are independent; i.e., if the word *aber* were removed, both clauses could function as sentences on their own.

NOTE: Coordinating conjunctions in German are:

aber	*but, however*
denn	*because*
oder	*or*
sondern	*but rather, but on the contrary*
und	*and*

When clauses are combined with one of these coordinating conjunctions, both clauses take regular word order. The finite verb, i.e., the part of the verb that takes endings, is the second element in each clause.

Wir schlagen unser Zelt schnell auf, denn wir wollen schwimmen gehen.

We are pitching our tent quickly because we want to go swimming.

Ich möchte schwimmen, aber meine Familie wandert lieber in den Bergen.

I would like to swim, but my family prefers to hike in the mountains.

Wir gehen nicht in die Stadt, sondern wir fahren aufs Land.

We're not going to the city, but rather we're going to the country.

ÜBUNG A   E-Gespräch. You are instant messaging with your German pen pal. He asks you questions about the Black Forest camping trip and you answer.

EXAMPLE: Hast du ein Zelt gekauft?

Ich habe eins gekauft, aber ich / das Zelt / nicht / mögen
Ich habe eins gekauft, aber ich mag das Zelt nicht.

1. Warum hast du das neue Zelt nicht gern? Ich mag es nicht, denn / es / zu klein / sein

   _____

2. Hast du neue Wanderschuhe gekauft? Ja, ich habe Schuhe gekauft / und / sie / prima / sein

   _____

3. Du sollst angeln gehen. Ich will angeln gehen, aber / vielleicht / ich / nicht genug / Zeit / haben

   _____

4. Warum hast du nicht genug Zeit? Ich will nicht nur angeln, sondern / ich / auch / viel wandern / möchten

   _____

5. Warum willst du so viel wandern? Ich will viel wandern, denn / die Wanderwege / um / der See / so gut / sein.

   _____

| ÜBUNG B | **Die Campingreise.** You and your friends are now planning a camping trip in your area. Discuss what you'd like to do including the suggested coordinating conjunctions in your responses. |

DEIN FREUND: Was tun wir auf der Campingreise? (und)

DU: Wir rudern auf dem See und wandern in den Bergen.

DEIN FREUND: Toll! Haben wir Zeit zum Baden? (aber)

DU: _____

DEIN FREUND: Schwimmst du gerne? (sondern)

_____

DEIN FREUND: Was machen wir abends? (oder)

_____

DEIN FREUND: Das wird Spaß machen! Kommt Gisela auch mit? (denn)

_____

2.   Subordinating Conjunctions

Subordinating conjunctions connect an independent with a dependent clause. The independent clause can stand alone as a complete sentence; the dependent clause usually cannot.

Bevor wir für den Schwarzfald abfahren, essen wir zusammen.

Before we depart for the Black Forest, we're eating together.

Common subordinating conjuntions are:

bevor	*before*
bis	*until*
damit	*so that*
dass	*that*
nachdem	*after*
ob	*if, whether*
obwohl	*although*
während	*while*
weil	*because*
***wenn**	*when, whenever*

wenn can also mean "if", but usually when used with the subjunctive form of the verb, which will not be introduced until level 3 of this series.

In clauses introduced by a subordinating conjunction, the verb goes to the end of the clause.

Ich esse immer ein Käsefondue, wenn ich in den Schwarzwald fahre.

I always eat cheese fondue whenever I go to the Black Forest.

Wir besuchen auch das Kuckucksuhrmuseum, während wir da sind.

We'll also visit the cuckoo clock museum while we're there.

If the finite verb has a separable prefix, then the stem and prefix are written together again when the verb goes to the end of a subordinating clause. In the sentences below, *hingehen* and *zuhören* are examples of separable prefixes that were reunited at the end of a subordinating clause.

Wir essen Samstag Abend früh, weil die Klasse um acht zum Folklore-Konzert hingeht.

We're eating early Saturday evening because the class is going to the folk concert at 8.

Obwohl ich gerne Volksmusik zuhöre, gehe ich nicht mit ins Konzert.

Although I like to listen to folk music, I'm not going along to the concert.

ÜBUNG C | **Ein Brief aus dem Schwarzwald.** Julian has written you again from the Black Forest. Write out the sentences to express what Julian does when he is in the Schwarzwald.

EXAMPLE: Ich esse immer Schwarzwälder Kirschtorte, wenn / ich / in / der Schwarzwald /
sein

Ich esse immer Schwarzwälder Kirschtorte, wenn ich im Schwarzwald bin.

1. Ich lese viel über die Gegend im Internet, bevor / ich / in / der Schwarzwald / fahren

   _____

2. Ich lerne viel, damit / ich / nichts / verpassen

   _____

3. Ich weiß, dass / es / unheimlich viel / in / die Gegend / zu sehen / geben

   _____

4. Ich esse immer viel, nachdem / ich / weit / in / die Berge / wandern

   _____

5. Ich singe mit, während / ich / am Lagerfeuer / sitzen

   _____

ÜBUNG D   **Einladung zum Campingausflug.** You enjoyed Julian's letter so much, that
you decided to plan your own camping trip. You've written an email to your
friends about it. Your copy machine, however, didn't make a very clean copy.
Add in the missing words from the following list:

bevor – bis – damit – dass   nachdem – obwohl   während – weil – wenn

Hallo, Freunde!

Während wir in den Sommerferien waren, hatte ich eine gute Idee. Jeden Sommer,

_____ ich mit meinen Eltern in den Bergen bin, gehe ich an einen kleinen See. Es ist

schön dort, _____ es kein Schwimmbad gibt. Ich glaube, _____ wir im

September sowieso nicht schwimmen können. Das Wetter ist zu kalt. Ich schreibe euch jetzt,

_____ ich uns einen Campingplatz reservieren kann, _____ wir nach Hause

fahren. _____ ich weiß, wieviel es kostet, schreibe ich euch wieder. Ich bin am

Montag nicht in der Schule, _____ meine Tante kommt. Also, ich kann kaum warten,

_____ wir uns am Dienstag sehen.

Euer Freund,

Axel

ÜBUNG E **Der Plan.** Your friends like the idea of a camping trip. You're about to have a planning meeting with them. You need to plan where you will go, who's sharing whose tent, etc. How do you think your friends will react to your statements? Write their reactions so that each answer has at least one clause (not just a single word) introduced by the given subordinating conjunction. You decide how cooperative your friends are going to be.

EXAMPLE: DU: Sarah, kannst du ein Zelt mit Johanna teilen?
SARAH: (aber) Ja, aber ich möchte lieber mit Rita teilen.

1. DU: Jessica, kannst du früher kommen und uns mit den Zelten helfen?
   JESSICA: (nachdem) _____

2. DU: Harry, kannst du mich abholen?
   HARRY: (obwohl) _____

3. DU: Emma, kannst du Würste für Samstag Abend bringen?
   EMMA: (sondern) _____

4. DU: Florian, warum willst du deinen Hund mitbringen?
   FLORIAN: (damit) _____

5. DU: Elke, kannst du das Lagerfeuer am Samstag Abend machen?
   ELKE: (weil) _____

6. DU: Wer hat noch eine Frage oder eine gute Idee?
   ELKE: (während) _____

7. EMMA: (ob) _____

8. FRANK: (bevor) _____

9. HARRY: (wenn) _____

10. Florian: (dass) _____

ÜBUNG F **Das Reisejournal.** The trip was a success. Hans, one of the students on the camping trip, kept a journal. Using the prompts, write down what he wrote.

EXAMPLE: Hans rollt seinen Schlafsack aus, bevor er ins Bett geht.

1. Hans löscht das Lagerfeuer, bevor er / ins Bett / gehen

   _____

2. Er liest nicht, während er / auf / die Campingreise / sein

   _____

3. Er mag Wandern, weil es / in / der Wald / sehr schön / sein

   _____

4. Er schläft viel, damit er / länger / wandern / können

   _____

5. Morgens wartet er im Zelt, bis die Sonne / aufgehen

   _____

6. Er steht dann auf, obwohl er / lieber / länger / schlafen

| ÜBUNG G | **Montagmorgens.** It is Monday after the trip and many of your classmates and even the teacher forgot to bring things to school. Think of some reasons why. |

EXAMPLE: Maja hat ihre Hausaufgaben nicht. Sie hat ihr Buch vergessen.
Maja hat ihre Hausaufgaben nicht, **weil** sie ihr Buch vergessen **hat.**

1. Kirsten hat keinen Kuli.

---

2. Gerd hat seine Schultasche nicht.

---

3. Maria und Susie haben ihre Sportkleider nicht.

---

4. Herr Petzhold hat seinen Kuli nicht.

---

3.   Word Order in Dependent Clauses with More than One Verb Element

Creating sentences with a dependent clause adds interest and variety to any text. Compound verb tenses, which also add interest, follow a defined pattern and are not difficult to use. The following rules define the various word order patterns.

a. Dependent Clauses in the Perfect Tense

The perfect tense has two elements, for example *hat gesagt* or *ist gefahren*. The finite verb (*hat* or *ist*) is the second element in a sentence and the past participle is at the end.

Er ist ins Folklore-Konzert gegangen.   *He went to the folklore concert.*

When that same sentence becomes a clause introduced by a subordinating conjunction, the finite verb goes to the end of the sentence.

Weisst du, ob er ins Folklore-Konzert gegangen ist?

Do you know if he went to the folklore concert?

Ich hoffe, dass Maria mit in den Schwarzwald gefahren ist.

I hope that Maria went with them to the Black Forest.

| ÜBUNG H | **Eine Email.** You decide to write your pen pal an e-mail. Add interest to it by using complex sentences. |

EXAMPLE: Gestern habe ich gelernt. (dass) Wir fahren in den Schwarzwald.
          Gestern haben ich gelernt, dass wir in den Schwarzwald fahren.

1. Ich habe gelesen. (dass) Das Schwarzwaldgebiet hat sehr viele Wandermöglichkeiten.

    _____

2. Wir werden zelten. (damit) Wir können den Wald wirklich genießen.

    _____

3. Ich weiß nicht. (ob) Mein neues Zelt ist groß genug.

    _____

4. Ich lese jeden Abend im Internet. (damit) Ich lerne viel über den Schwarzwald.

    _____

5. Ich wandere gerne. (wenn) Ich habe die richtigen Schuhe dazu.

    _____

| ÜBUNG I | **Die Aufgabenliste.** While on your camping trip different people do things to help out. Write the story to express what they do.

EXAMPLE: Katrina / mit dem Zelt / helfen / wollen / bevor / sie / schwimmen gehen
          Katrina will mit dem Zelt helfen, bevor sie schwimmen geht.

1. Margot / das erste Abendessen / kochen / weil / sie / gut / kochen / können

    _____

2. Wir / Margot / helfen / damit / das Essen / schnell / fertig / werden

    _____

3. Wir / immer / interessante Geschichten/ erzählen / während / wir / essen

    _____

4. Wir / immer / viel / essen / weil / wir / dauernd / Hunger / haben

    _____

5. Wir / jeden Tag / essen / bis / es / nichts mehr / geben

    _____

b. Dependent Clauses with Modal Verbs

The same rule applies if there is a modal verb in a dependent clause. The modal goes to the end of the clause behind its completer.

Below are two independent statements. They can be combined using *ob* to form a single-sentence question.

Er hat gesagt.   Er kann morgen kommen. (ob)
He said.   He can come tomorrow.

ÜBUNG J   **Weißt du, ob . . .?** Combine the two sentences using the conjunction *ob*.

NOTE: In English one says "I don't know." In German, this sentence is *Ich weiß es nicht.* When there is a completing clause, the *es* is dropped.

EXAMPLE: Wir wissen (es) nicht. Wir alle essen Fisch gern.
    Wir wissen nicht, ob wir alle Fisch gern essen.

1. Er will (es) wissen. Wir essen zwei oder drei Würste pro Person.

   _____

2. Meine Mutter will (es) wissen. Kommen wir am Sonntag oder Montag zurück?

   _____

3. Herr Marzipan hat gesagt. Er bleibt das ganze Wochenende bei uns.

   _____

4. Ich weiß (es) nicht. Fahren wir am Donnerstag oder Freitag Abend ab?

   _____

In the combined sentence, the modal goes to the end beyond its completer.

Hat er gesagt, ob er morgen kommen kann?

Did he say whether he can come tomorrow?

Wir müssen das Zelt aufschlagen, bevor wir in die Stadt gehen dürfen.

We have to set up the tent before we are allowed to go into town.

ÜBUNG K   **Majas Fragen.** Maja is a persistent person and always asks questions. She wants to know if you know.

EXAMPLE: Weißt du, ob / wir / morgen/ dürfen / angeln
    Weißt du, ob wir morgen angeln dürfen

1. wir / immer im Zelt / schlafen / müssen

   _____

2. wir / unsere Schlafsäcke /sollen / mitbringen

   _____

3. du / dein altes Zelt / wollen / mitbringen

   _____

4. ich / ab und zu / dürfen / kochen

   _____

5. Fritz / ein Lagerfeuer / jeden Abend / können / machen

   _____

ÜBUNG L   **Die Fotobeschreibungen.** You are writing to your friend about your classmates. Use the pictures from the camping trip to tell what you know about them.

EXAMPLE: Ich weiss, dass Agnes gut Fussball spielen kann.

1. Ich weiß, dass Dirk

2. Ich habe nicht gewusst, dass Gerda _____

3. Ich weiß, dass Viktor

4. Ich weiss, dass Uwe _____

5. Ich habe nicht gewusst, dass Anika _____

| ÜBUNG M | **Bevor du hingehst . . .** Combine the sentence elements with the first part of the sentence to express what Frau Martin tells her child Josef to do before the camping trip. |

EXAMPLE: Du musst dein Frühstück essen, bevor / du /wandern / gehen
Du musst dein Frühstück essen, bevor du wandern gehst.

1. Du sollst deine Badehose mitnehmen, wenn / du / schwimmen / wollen

   _____

2. Zeig mir dein Aufgabenheft, damit / ich / die Auskunft / von Herrn Marzipan / sehen / können!

   _____

3. Ich verstehe, dass / du / ein Zelt / mit / Josef / teilen / wollen

   _____

4. Du musst alle deine Aufgaben machen, bevor / du / in den Schwarzwald / fahren / dürfen

   _____

5. Weißt du, ob / du / deine Gitarre mitnehmen / dürfen?

   _____

4. Interrogatives as Subordinating Conjunctions

Question words act as subordinating conjunctions when they are used to combine two clauses.

Wissen Sie, wann wir abfahren sollen? *Do you know when we are supposed to leave?*

Habt ihr gesehen, wo das Eiscafé ist? *Did you see where the ice cream parlor is?*

Kannst du mir bitte erklären, wie man ein Zelt aufschlägt? *Can you please explain to me, how one sets up a tent?*

| ÜBUNG N | **Fragen.** You are talking with the twins Gerda and Gerlinde and have several questions about the upcoming camping trip. Ask them questions using at least 5 of the interrogatives *wer, wie, was, wann, wie viel, wie viele* and *warum*. |

NOTE: Use *wie viele* if the quantity can be counted, *wie viel* if it can't.

EXAMPLE: Wisst ihr, wie viel Geld wir bringen sollen?

1. _____

2. _____

3. _____

4. _____

5. _____

| ÜBUNG O | **Unsere Campingreise.** You write your pen pal asking about what the teacher said about your upcoming trip.

EXAMPLE: Hat Herr Marzipan gesagt, dass / wir / Neustadt / besuchen / können?
Hat Herr Marzipan gesagt, dass wir Neustadt besuchen können?

1. Hat er gesagt, ob / wir / immer / auf / das Land / bleiben?

_____

2. Hat er gesagt, wann / wir / er / das Geld / geben / sollen?

_____

3. Hat er erklärt, wie / wir / in / der Schwarzwald / fahren / sollen?

_____

4. Hat er eine Ahnung, wie viel / Geld / wir / mitbringen / sollen?

_____

5. Weiß er, dass / wir / alle / schon / unsere Zelte / kaufen (present perfect)?

_____

5. Inverted Word Order with Introductory Subordinate Clauses

In German sometimes the dependent clause, the one which cannot stand alone, goes before the independent clause. The whole clause then becomes the first element in the sentence. The finite verb goes to the end of its clause, and the second finite verb starts the next clause.

Wenn ich mit meinen Freunden zelte, bringe ich immer eine Taschenlampe mit.

Whenever I go camping with my friends, I always bring a flashlight along.

Nachdem wir das Museum besichtigt haben, gehen wir in ein Eiscafé.

After we have visited the museum, we'll go to an ice cream parlor.

Damit wir alle ins Museum reinkommen können, gebe ich euch eure Eintrittskarten.

So that we can all get into the museum, I'll give you your entrance tickets.

| ÜBUNG P | **Das Telefongespräch.** You receive a phone call telling you about the plans for your trip. Try to remember what was said based on your notes.

EXAMPLE: damit / wir / keine Probleme / haben, / alle Schüler / ein Schlafsack / vor Mai / brauchen

Damit wir keine Probleme haben, brauchen alle Schüler einen Schlafsack vor Mai.

1. wenn / wir / reisen, / alle Schüler / immer / zusammenbleiben / sollen

_____

2. weil / wir / nicht viel / Zeit / haben, / wir / nicht alles / sehen / können

_____

3. wann / wir / schwimmen gehen / können, / wir / noch nicht / wissen

_____

4. ob / wir / immer / nur / auf dem Campingplatz / essen, / wir / besprechen / müssen

_____

5. dass / wir / gut / sich benehmen / sollen, / alle Schüler / klar / sein

_____

NOTE: Experimenting with complex sentences and combining smaller sentences into longer ones are excellent stylistic devices. The resulting German sounds more natural and sophisticated. It becomes even more fluid and interesting with the use of compound verb forms and varying word order. The rules are the same regardless of the length or complexity of the sentence:

1. The finite verb always goes to the end of its clause if the clause is introduced with a subordinating conjunction.

2. The finite verb is always the second element in its sentence or in an independent clause introduced by a coordinating conjunction.

| ÜBUNG Q | **Unsere Campingreise.** Write a story about your recent camping trip. Incorporate at least six of the conjunctions below into the story. Remember to check if the conjunction is coordinating or subordinating. Use interesting vocabulary. |

aber, oder, sondern, bevor, damit, dass, ob, obwohl, während, weil, wenn

_____

_____

_____

_____

_____

_____

_____

_____

_____

CHAPTER 12
Modal Verbs

1. Formation of the Modal Verbs

Modal verbs allow you to express ability, permission, desire, obligation or necessity. There are only six modal verbs:

dürfen, darf	*may, be permitted to, to be allowed to*
können, kann	*can, be able to*
mögen, mag	*like, like to*
müssen, muss	*must, have to*
sollen, soll	*should, ought to, supposed to*
wollen, will	*want*

All modal verbs except *sollen* require a vowel change from the singular to the plural. Their conjugation in the present tense is:

MODAL VERBS – PRESENT TENSE						
	DÜRFEN to be permitted to, allowed to, may	**KÖNNEN** to be able to, can	**MÖGEN** to like to, like	**MÜSSEN** to have to, must	**SOLLEN** to be supposed to, ought to, should	**WOLLEN** to want to, want
ich	darf	kann	mag	muss	soll	will
du	darfst	kannst	magst	musst	sollst	willst
er,sie, es	darf	kann	mag	muss	soll	will
wir	dürfen	können	mögen	müssen	sollen	wollen
ihr	dürft	könnt	mögt	müsst	sollt	wollt
sie	dürfen	können	mögen	müssen	sollen	wollen
Sie	dürfen	können	mögen	müssen	sollen	wollen

2.   Word Order of Modal Verbs

Modal verbs usually need a completer. A modal used alone leaves too many questions unanswered.

In order to complete the meaning of a sentence a final infinitive is added.

Kannst du ein Lagerfeuer machen?   *Can you make a campfire?*

Ich mag nicht wandern, weil mir meine Füsse immer weh tun.

I don't like to hike because my feet always hurt.

ÜBUNG A   **Du sollst nicht . . .** You are planning your trip. Use the sentence elements to express what your teacher tells you.

EXAMPLE: du / ein Zelt / besorgen / müssen   Du musst ein Zelt besorgen.

1. du / keine Bankkarte / mitbringen / sollen

   _____

2. wir / meistens / auf dem Land / bleiben / müssen

   _____

3. du / auch / gute Wanderschuhe / haben / müssen

   _____

4. du / vielleicht / neue Kleider / kaufen / wollen

   _____

5. du / ein Schlafsack / kaufen / können

   _____

6. ihr / fast / jeden Abend / ein Lagerfeuer / machen / dürfen

   _____

ÜBUNG B   **Muttis Worte.** Your mother also gives you suggestions for your trip.

EXAMPLE: Du sollst gut essen.

genug schlafen	*sollen*
dein Tagebuch mitnehmen	*können*
mir eine Karte schreiben	*sollen*
gut essen	*sollen*
brav sein	*wollen*
dein Teddybär mitbringen?	*müssen*

1. _____

2. _____

3. _____

4. _____

5. _____

Like all finite verbs, the modal is usually the second element. Its infinitive completer is at the end of the clause or sentence. If the clause is introduced by a subordinate conjunction, the finite verb goes to the end of the sentence after the completer.

> **Ich hoffe. Ich kann ins Kino gehen. (dass)**
>
> **Ich hoffe, dass ich ins Kino gehen kann.**   *I hope (that) I can go to the movies.*

Combining the two sentences was accomplished by using the subordinating conjunction *dass* (that) and moving the finite verb to the end of its clause.

> **Mein Bruder darf mitkommen, wenn er den Film sehen will.**
>
> *My brother is permitted to come along if he wants to see the movie.*

ÜBUNG C   **Du kannst nur kommen, wennt . . .** Your teacher puts restrictions on a planned class outing. Match the columns to express what you teacher says.

EXAMPLE: Du musst gute Noten haben, wenn du mitfahren willst.

du / gute Noten / haben / müssen	ob / ihr / mit / wir / in die Stadt / fahren / dürfen
ihr / noch nicht / wissen	wenn / du / mitfahren / wollen
wir / hoffen	dass / wir / jeden Abend / ein Lagerfeuer / machen / können
ihr / wissen	dass / wir / nicht / in / das Kino / gehen / wollen
ich / hoffen	dass / alle / mitkommen / dürfen

1. _____

2. _____

3. _____

4. _____

3.   Modal Verbs in the Present Perfect Tense

Modals are often used in the present perfect tense.

Ich habe nicht gehen dürfen.   *I was not permitted to go.*

a. Present Perfect Modals with no Completer

All modal verbs use *haben* as an auxiliary verb. The participles all start with *ge-* and end with a *–t*.

MODAL VERBS PRESENT PERFECT TENSE		
MODAL	PRESENT PERFECT TENSE	ENGLISH MEANING
dürfen	hat . . . gedurft	*has been allowed, was allowed*
können	hat . . . gekonnt	*has been able to, was able to, could*
mögen	hat . . . gemocht	*has liked to, has liked, liked, liked to*
müssen	hat . . . gemusst	*has had to, had to*
sollen	hat . . . gesollt	*was supposed to*
wollen	hat . . . gewollt	*has wanted to, wanted to, wanted*

The modal verb used without an infinitive completer follows the established rules of word order, i.e. the auxiliary verb *haben* is in the second position and the past participle is at the end of the clause.

Ich habe einen neuen Computer gewollt.   *I wanted a new computer.*

Ich habe Spanisch gemocht, aber jetzt mag ich Deutsch lieber.

I liked Spanish, but now I prefer German.

ÜBUNG D | **Omas Erinnerungen.** You've been listening to your grandmother tell stories about her childhood. Life was certainly different when you were that age. Create comparisons using the suggested modals and following the given sentence pattern.

EXAMPLE: Als Oma 10 Jahre alt war, hat sie ein Fahrrad gewollt.
Als ich 10 Jahre alt war, habe ich ein Motorskateboard gewollt.

Pferdereiten? Als Oma zehn Jahre alt war, hat sie das gekonnt.
Pferdereiten? Als ich zehn Jahre alt war, habe ich das nicht gekonnt.

1. Als Oma zehn Jahre alt war, hat sie die Beatles gemocht.

   _____

2. Allein in die Stadt laufen? Als Oma zehn Jahre alt war, hat sie das gedurft.

   _____

3. Schwimmen? Als Oma zehn Jahre alt war, hat sie das nicht gekonnt.

   _____

4. Als Oma zehn Jahre alt war, hat sie einen Farbfernseher gewollt.

   _____

5. Jeans in der Schule tragen? Als Oma zehn Jahre alt war, hat sie das nicht gedurft.

   _____

b. Present Perfect Modals with a Completer

Most often modals are used with an infinitive completer. In that case, the clause ends in two infinitives.

Present Tense: **Ich kann kommen**   *I can come.*

Present Perfect Tense: **Ich habe kommen können.**   *I was able to come. I could come.*

Ich habe nicht hingehen wollen.   *I didn't want to go.*

Mein Bruder hat nicht mitkommen wollen.   *My brother did not want to come.*

Modals used in the present perfect have three components: the finite verb (a form of *haben*), the infinitive completer, and the modal which is also used in the infinitive.

Das Haus war so laut, ihr habt nicht   lernen   können.
            verb   infinitive completer   modal

The house was so loud, you weren't able to study.

The easiest way to remember the word order is VIM – verb, infinitive, modal.

ÜBUNG E   **Omas Zeiten.** You were so interested in your grandmother's stories that you want to ask her more questions about her childhood. Prepare your sentences, this time using infinitive completers. You should create one sentence for each modal.

EXAMPLE: Oma, hast du mit 16 Jahren rauchen dürfen?

1. dürfen _____

2. können _____

3. mögen _____

4. müssen _____

5. sollen _____

6. wollen _____

ÜBUNG F   **Fotos von Oma.** Your grandmother answered your questions. She's also sent you some pictures of her as a very young child. Use the pictures to describe what she could do as a young child. Use the suggested modal and an infinitive completer.

EXAMPLE: Sie hat im Sandkisten spielen können.

1. müssen _____

2. dürfen _____

3. können _____

4. wollen _____

5. sollen _____

6. mögen _____

ÜBUNG G **Dürfen und nicht dürfen.** You are writing your pen pal about the restrictions during your last class trip.

EXAMPLE: nicht alleine fahren   Ich habe nicht alleine fahren dürfen.

1. nicht ohne einen Partner durch die Straßen laufen

_____

2. nicht bei McDonald's essen

_____

3. nicht / in /der Kaufhof / gehen

_____

4. nicht / mit / fremde Leuten / sprechen

_____

5. nicht / nach 22.00 Uhr / auf die Straße / gehen

_____

4. Present Perfect Modals in a Subordinate Clause

VIM (verb-infinitive-modal) is the proper word order for the three parts of a modal verb in the present perfect tense.

Ich habe ihn anrufen müssen. _I had to call him up._
verb   infinitive   modal

NOTE: Nothing changes when the present perfect modal with completer occurs in a subordinate clause. The finite verb goes to the end of its clause, but before the infinitive and modal. The VIM word order is maintained.

Simple Sentence: **Er hat nicht kommen können.**   _He wasn't able to come._
                                     verb   infinitive   modal
Subordinate Clause: **Weißt du, dass er nicht hat kommen können?**
                                                       verb infinitive   modal
                                     Did you know that he wasn't able to come?

ÜBUNG H | **Ungerecht!** One of your classmates claims that the rules for the trip were not fair. Use the rules from _Übung G_ to express what he claims.

EXAMPLE: Es ist nicht fair, dass / wir / bei McDonald's / nicht / essen / dürfen
                    Es war nicht fair, dass wir bei McDonald's nicht haben essen dürfen!

1. Es war unrecht, dass _____

2. Ich fand es komisch, dass _____

3. Ich konnte es nicht glauben, dass _____

4. Ich verstehe nicht, warum _____

5. Weißt du, warum _____

ÜBUNG I | **Aber doch nötig.** You answer his complaints by giving reasons why the regulations were necessary. Match the reasons with the regulations.

EXAMPLE: Weil die Schule für uns dann keine Autoversicherung hat, haben wir nicht alleine fahren dürfen.

1. Damit wir alleine nicht verloren gegangen sind,

   _____

2. Damit wir oft die gute, schwäbische Küche im Schwarzwald probiert haben,

   _____

3. Damit wir unser Geld nicht zu schnell ausgegeben haben,

   _____

4. Damit uns nichts Schlechtes passiert ist,

   _____

5. Damit wir alle jeden Abend ins Jugendhotel gekommen sind,

   _____

| ÜBUNG J | **Letzten Sommer.** Last summer while you were on vacation there were many things that you were able to do or allowed to do. List five of those activities and the reasons you could do them in the summer. |

EXAMPLE: Ich habe oft schwimmen können, weil es sehr warm war.
Ich habe bis Mitternacht aufbleiben dürfen, weil es keine Schule gab.

1. _____

2. _____

3. _____

4. _____

5. _____

CHAPTER 13
Adjectives

1. Weak Adjective Endings

Adjectives preceding a noun have three types of endings: weak, strong or mixed (See chapter 6).

Adjectives which follow a definite article (*der-die-das*) take weak adjective endings:

				PLURAL
WEAK ADJECTIVE ENDINGS *after a* DEFINITE ARTICLE				
	SINGULAR			PLURAL
		FEMININE		MASCULINE
NOMINATIVE	der alt-e	die alt-e	das alt-e	die alt-en
DATIVE	dem alt-en	der alt-en	dem alt-en	den alt-en
ACCUSATIVE	den alt-en	die alt-e	das alt-e	die alt-en

ÜBUNG A   **Noch gut?** Maria is taking stock of her camping equipment. Write out the sentences to express her problems.

EXAMPLE: die / alt____ Wanderstiefel / ich / nicht mehr / passen
Die alten Wanderstiefel passen mir nicht mehr.

1. ich / das klein___ Zelt / gebrauchen / wollen

   _____

2. ich / nicht mehr /mit / der gebrochen____ Wanderstock / wandern

   _____

3. Ich / nicht gut / in / der gestreift____ Pulli / aussehen

   _____

4. ich / die ält____ Wanderhose / ersetzen / wollen

   _____

5. der schön____, alt____ Regenmantel / kaputt /sein

   _____

6. die dick____ Strümpfe / viele Löcher / haben

_____

7. die braun____ Shorts / ich / auch / nicht mehr / passen

_____

2.   Demonstrative Adjectives

There are six words that take the same endings as the definite article _der/die/das_.

DEMONSTRATIVE ADJECTIVES				
	SINGULAR			PLURAL
	MASCULINE	FEMININE	NEUTER	
NOMINATIVE	**dieser**	**diese**	**dieses**	**diese**
DATIVE	**diesem**	**dieser**	**diesem**	**diesen**
ACCUSATIVE	**diesen**	**diese**	**dieses**	**diese**

The words are:

dieser – _this, these_
jener - _that, those_
jeder (plural **alle**) –
each, every (plural _all_)

*mancher – _some_
*solcher – _such a, such_
welcher – _which_
*used most commonly in the plural

Manche Leute campen nicht gerne.   _Some people don't like to camp._

Diese Klasse zeltet aber sehr gerne.   _This class however likes to camp in tents._

In welchem Zelt schläfst du?   _In which tent are you sleeping?_

| ÜBUNG B | **Was hast du gern?** Tina and Tilman are shopping for the camping trip. As they pick up articles they express their liking for them.

EXAMPLE: Ich habe diesen Pulli gern.

1. _____

2. _____

3. _____

4. _____

5. _____

ÜBUNG C | **Was magst du lieber?** Your pen pal will be visiting you and you want to find out what things she likes. Write out the questions based on the pictures.

EXAMPLE: Welches Getränk magst du? Cola oder Milch?

1. _____

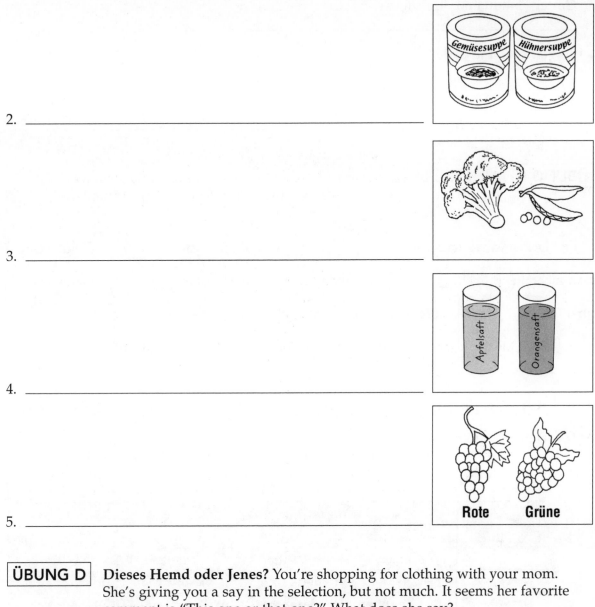

2. _____

3. _____

4. _____

5. _____

| ÜBUNG D | **Dieses Hemd oder Jenes?** You're shopping for clothing with your mom. She's giving you a say in the selection, but not much. It seems her favorite comment is "This one or that one?" What does she say? |

EXAMPLE: Hemd? Magst du dieses rote Hemd oder jenes Blaue?

NOTE: Since the GNC and context make it obvious that you are talking about shirts, you do not have to repeat the word *Hemd*. Capitalizing the final adjective signals that there is a noun missing, i.e. that the final adjective is standing in for the entire adjective-noun combination.

1. Tennisschuhe – weiß und schwarz

_____

2. Sonntagshose – braun und dunkelblau

_____

3. Gürtel – braun und dunkelblau

_____

4. Socken – rot und blau

_____

5. T-Shirt – hellgrün und hellblau

_____

| **ÜBUNG E** | **Alle?** Your friend is complaining loudly about the shopping trip with his mother. Fill in his comments with the correct forms of *jeder* (plural *alle*), *mancher* and *solcher*. |

Alle Jacken waren hässlich. _____ Schuh war altmodisch. _____ Schuhe trägt

man nicht mehr! Nicht _____ Hemden waren schlecht, aber _____ waren

furchtbar. _____ Hose war zu breit. Und _____ Krawatte war zu dünn.

_____ Mütter können gut für ihre Söhne einkaufen, aber meine nicht!

3.   Adjective Endings Following a Demonstrative Adjective

NOTE: A demonstrative adjective functions exactly like the definite article *der-die-das*. Adjectives sandwiched between a demonstrative adjective and a noun take the same weak adjective endings they would if they followed a *der*-word.

WEAK ADJECTIVE ENDINGS *after a* DEMONSTRATIVE ADJECTIVE				
	SINGULAR			PLURAL
	MASCULINE	FEMININE	NEUTER	
NOMINATIVE	dieser rot-e	diese rot-e	dieses rot-e	diese rot-en
DATIVE	diesem rot-en	dieser rot-en	diesem rot-en	diesen rot-en
ACCUSATIVE	diesen rot-en	diese rot-e	dieses rot-e	die jung-en

Marta, du bist in diesem gelben Zelt, und Sonia, du bist in jenem roten Zelt.
Marta, you are in this yellow tent, and Sonia, you are in that red tent.

Jedes Buch in dieser hochinteressanten Harry Potter Reihe ist lesenswert.
Every book in this highly interesting Harry Potter series is worthy of reading.

| **ÜBUNG F** | **Einkaufen in der Campingabteilung.** You are in the camping department of the local department store and hear only half of a conversation well. What do you think Steffi answered? |

EXAMPLE: Stefan - Welchen Pulli magst du?

Steffi – ich / dies____ / rot ____ / Pulli / mögen

_____

Stefan – Wie findest du solche grünen Wanderschuhe?

Steffi – solch____ / grün____ / Wanderschuhe / modisch / sein

_____

Stefan – Jedes Zelt hier sieht gleich aus.

Steffi – Nein / jen____ / blau____ / Zelt / dort drüben /ganz / anders / sein

_____

Stefan – Möchten wir dieses blaue Zelt kaufen?

Steffi – ich / glauben / dass / dies____ / blau____ / Zelt / zu viel / kosten

_____

Stefan – Welchen Schlafsack willst du haben?

Steffi – Ich / es / nicht / wissen / manch____ dick____ Schlafsäcke / zu dick / sein

_____

ÜBUNG G   **Opas Meinung.** Your grandfather is a man who thinks that the old days were much better. He has opinions about everything. What do you think he says about the following? Then add four others he might say.

EXAMPLE: Solche großen Autos mag ich nicht.
            Solche jungen Leute haben kein gutes Benehmen.

1. Solche alten Leute _____

2. Solche dummen Politiker _____

3. _____

4. _____

5. _____

6. _____

ÜBUNG H   **Aber Opa!** You disagree with the things your grandfather said. Write replies where you claim that many of the things are good.

EXAMPLE: Aber manche großen Autos sind sehr schön.
          Aber manche junge Leute benehmen sich sehr gut.

_____

_____

_____

_____

_____

ÜBUNG I   **Eine Email.** You printed out an e-mail from your pen pal but you spilled some soup on it. Fill in the missing words. The words are forms of demonstrative adjectives or articles paired with descriptive adjectives.

Hallo,

du weißt schon, dass manch _____ jung_____ Schüler nicht gern wandern. Und du?

Bist du einer von dies _____ faul _____ Typen? Ich hoffe nicht. Hast du ein gutes

Zelt? Gott sei dank ist jed_____ gut _____ Zelt heutzutage wasserdicht. Bei manch

_____ billig _____ Zelten wirst du nass, wenn du solch _____ regnerisch

_____ Wetter hast, wie im Frühling ganz normal ist. Ich wünsche dir viel Spaß und ein

solch _____ Wetter, dass du kein _____ Regenschirm brauchst.

Micky

4. Mixed Adjective Endings

Adjectives which follow an indefinite article take mixed adjective endings.

WEAK ADJECTIVE ENDINGS *after an* INDEFINITE ARTICLE			
	SINGULAR		PLURAL
	MASCULINE	FEMININE	NEUTER	
NOMINATIVE	ein alt-er	eine alt-e	ein alt-es	meine alt-en
DATIVE	einem alt-en	einer alt-en	einem alt-en	meinen alt-en
ACCUSATIVE	einen alt-en	eine alt-e	ein alt-es	meine alt-en

The words that follow this pattern (see list on following page) are *ein, kein,* and all the possessive adjectives.

ein	*a, an*		sein	*his*
kein	*none, not any, no*		**unser**	*our, ours*
mein	*my, mine*		**euer**	*your, yours (informal plural)*
dein	*your, yours (informal singular)*		**ihr**	*their, theirs*
sein	*its*		**Ihr**	*your, yours (formal)*
ihr	*her, hers*			

ÜBUNG J | **Wessen?** Lorenzo found a box of clothing in his closet that must have been packed last year. He leaves a note to his family asking to whom the articles belong.

EXAMPLE: Mutti, ist das deine gelbe Bluse?

Mutti	die gelbe Bluse
Vati	die blauen Hemden
Marco	der braune Gürtel
Mutti und Vati	die dicken Winterschale
Maria	die schwarze Hose
Mutti	die beigen Schuhe
Marco	der alte Mantel
Marco und Maria	die schmutzigen Stiefel

1. _____

2. _____

3. _____

4. _____

5. _____

6. _____

7. _____

ÜBUNG K | **Ein Kartenspiel.** You are playing a game with your younger sister. She is supposed to answer questions based on pictures on cards, but is being difficult and only claiming to see one item of two pictured items. Write the questions and her answers. Follow the pattern in the example.

EXAMPLE: Siehst du ein weißes und ein schwarzes Auto?
Nein, ich sehe nur das schwarze Auto.

1. _____

_____

2. _____

_____

3. _____

_____

4. _____

_____

seine   ihre

5. _____

_____

5.   The Adjective Used as a Noun

Often the noun following a *der*-word or an *ein*-word is so obvious that it is left out. To leave it in would be repetitive.

Mama, du bist die Beste!	*Mom, you are the best (mom)!*
Das Gelbe dort ist mein Zelt.	*The yellow (tent) over there is my tent.*
Möchtest du ein Glas Limo?	*Would you like a glass of soda?*
Ja, ein Großes bitte.	*Yes, a large (glass of soda) please.*

NOTE: If the noun is eliminated, the articles and adjectives take exactly the same endings they would have if the noun were there. The descriptive adjective is capitalized to show that it's taking the place of the missing noun.

ÜBUNG L   **Ja, ein Rotes bitte**. You and your friend are looking at an online catalog. Answer the questions by referring to the color, size, etc. of the item you like.

EXAMPLE: Hast du die Hemden gern?   rot
Ja, ich habe das Rote gern.

1. Hast du die Jeanshosen gern?   blau

   _____

2. Hast du die Jacken gern?   schwarz

   _____

3. Magst du die Wanderstiefel?   schwer

   _____

4. Wie findest du die Zelten?   groß

   _____

5. Magst du die Gürtel?   braun

   _____

ÜBUNG M   **Der Persönlichkeitstest.** You are taking one of those personality tests online. You must choose which of the two things in the picture you prefer.

EXAMPLE: Ich habe den Kleinen lieber.

1. _____

2. _____

3. _____

4. _____

5. _____

NOTE: The noun is also often eliminated if it's *Mann* or *Frau*. *Der Kranke* is the sick man. The word *Mann* is not necessary. If you look at the chart above, *der Kranke* can only be masculine, singular and nominative. The endings are so strong, that the word *Mann* is understood.

> **Die Arme braucht Hilfe.**   *The poor (woman) needs help.*
>
> **Der Große dort drüben ist mein Bruder.**   *The tall (man) over there is my brother.*
>
> **Fährst du mit jenem Kranken ins Krankenhaus mit?**
>
> *Are you riding to the hospital with that sick (man)?*

ÜBUNG N   Die Testfortsetzung . . . . Now you are taking the second part of the personality test. This part deals with people and you must choose the one you like the best . . . the man, the woman, or the child.

EXAMPLE: Der Traurige gefällt mir am besten.

1. _____

2. _____

3. _____

4. _____

5. _____

| ÜBUNG O | **Alleine Einkaufen.** You won. Your mother is allowing you to go clothes shopping on your own, but first you have to show your mother what you like and don't like. You decide to print some outfits from the Internet and comment on them so that she begins to understand your style. Use each of the following words at least once: |

alle – dieser – jeder – jener – mancher – solcher – welcher

_____

_____

_____

_____

_____

_____

_____

_____

_____

CHAPTER 14
Adverbs

1.   Adverbs

Adverbs modify a verb, an adjective, or another adverb. They answer the question "when," "how," "where" and "to what extent." Most adverbs in English can easily be recognized because they end in -ly. German is even less complicated. An adverb never takes an ending.

Karl fährt langsam und sicher in die Stadt.   *Karl drives slowly and carefully into town.*
Sei brav! Sei still, mein Kind!   *Be good! Be quiet, my child!*

| ÜBUNG A | **Du über dich.** Tell the class about yourself by answering the following questions. You may use more than one sentence in your answer. Be positive and creative. Your teacher may ask you to share your answers with the class. |

EXAMPLE: Wie schreibst du? Ich schreibe schnell (akkurat / kreativ / gern / unlesbar.)
Wie bist du, wenn du traurig bist? Ich weine viel und bin unglücklich.

1. Wie bist du, wenn du freundlich bist?

   _____

2. Wie singst du, wenn du unter der Dusche bist?

   _____

3. Wie liest du, wenn du etwas für die Schule lesen musst?

   _____

4. Wie bist du, wenn du unzufrieden (= unsatisfied) bist?

   _____

5. Wie bist du, wenn du einen sehr großen Hund siehst?

   _____

2. Adverbs in Categories

It's easy to recognize most adverbs. Some are unique and need to be learned. The following two lists are common adverbs that will add to the ability to express yourself more exactly in German.

a. Common Adverbs of Time

morgens	*in the morning*
nachmittags	*in the afternoon*
abends	*in the evening*
nachts	*in the night*
montags	*on Mondays*
vorher	*before*
danach	*afterwards*
vorgestern	*the day before yesterday*
gestern	*yesterday*
heute	*today*
morgen	*tomorrow*
übermorgen	*the day after tomorrow*
spät	*late*
früh	*early*
schon	*already*
jetzt, nun	*now*
bald	*soon*
dann	*then*
gleich	*at once*
gleichzeitig	*at the same time*
sofort	*immediately*
immer	*always*
nie	*never*
manchmal	*sometimes*
täglich	*daily*
ab und zu	*occasionally*

ÜBUNG B | **Was lesen Sie?** You survey the librarian about students' reading habits. Use your notes which you wrote in columns to write a report.

EXAMPLE: Die Fünfklässler lesen immer Bilderbücher.

Die Fünfklässler	← lesen	täglich	die Zeitung
Die Sechsklässler	immer	→ Bilderbücher
Die Siebtklässler	schon	Geschichten über Magier
Die Achtklässler	nie	etwas
Die Neuntklässler	jetzt viel	von Cornelia Funke
Die Zehntklässler	manchmal	Harry Potter

1. _____

2. _____

3. _____

4. _____

5. _____

ÜBUNG C   **Jetzt bist du dran.** Now it's your turn. Each of you has been assigned a fifth grader to interview. Choose what you want to know about your student, and then create your questions. The only rule is that each question be answered using adverbs from the list above. Remember, an adverb answers in one word the following questions: "where," "when," "how," and "to what extent." When you're done, write down the answers you expect to get from your student.

EXAMPLE: Wann machst du deine Hausaufgaben?
Ich mache sie **sofort**, nachdem ich nach Hause komme.

1. _____

_____

2. _____

_____

3. _____

_____

4. _____

_____

5. _____

_____

ÜBUNG D   **Die Trainingsroutinen.** You are training for your camping trip. Each student does a different type of exercise at a different time. Use the pictures to write about your classmates.

EXAMPLE: morgens   Morgens joggt Karl.

1. früh am Morgen _____

2. jeden Tag _____

3. montags _____

4. manchmal _____

5. täglich _____

b. Common Adverbs of Manner, Place and Quantity

gern	*gladly*
ungern	*not gladly*
natürlich	*naturally*
selbstverständlich	*of course*
vielleicht	*maybe*
möglicherweise	*possibly*
wahrscheinlich	*probably*
hier	*here*
dort, da	*there*
dort drüben	*over there*
rechts	*to the right*
links	*to the left*
geradeaus	*straight ahead*
eigentlich	*actually*
sehr	*very*
oft	*often*
selten	*seldom*
ganz	*totally*
leider	*unfortunately*
teilweise	*partly*
schnell	*fast*
langsam	*slow*
vorsichtig	*carefully*

ÜBUNG E | **Dein Sport-Ich.** You are answering a questionnaire about your athletic endeavors. You must write how, where, when or how much you participate. Choose five of the activities listed or use others you know in German and use the adverbs from the list above.

Fussball, Baskettball, Handball, Volleyball, usw., spielen
schwimmen, reiten, wandern, Rad fahren, Skateboard fahren,

EXAMPLE: Ich fahre selten Skateboard.

1. _____

2. _____

3. _____

4. _____

5. _____

ÜBUNG F   **Die Verkehrsschilder.** Show your understanding of German traffic signs.
How and where must you drive?

EXAMPLE: Du sollst rechts fahren.

1. _____

2. _____

3. _____

4. _____

5. _____

3.   **Word Order of Adverbs and Adverbial Phrases**

When two or more adverbs or adverbial phrases are used in the same sentence, they should be in the TMP order (time, manner and place). Any of these three elements may be used as the first element in the sentence if you wish to emphasize it. If that is the case, then the verb comes next as the second element and the remaining adverbs or adverbial phrases are in the TMP order.

Mittags macht er immer seine Hausaufgaben mit seiner Mutter in der Küche.
   time   time   manner   place

| ÜBUNG G | **Der Fernwanderer.** You interviewed a German-speaking long-distance hiker. Now you need to write an article for the school newspaper. Use your notes. Make sure your modifiers are in TMP word order. Add interest to your writing by starting your sentences with something other than the word *er*. |

EXAMPLE: Herr Wanderer / jeden Tag / in dem Park / vorsichtig / trainieren
               Herr Wanderer trainiert jeden Tag vorsichtig im Park.

1. er / schnell / oft / durch den Park / spazieren

   _____

2. er / manchmal / mit seinem Hund / montags / gehen

   _____

3. er / immer / geradeaus / meistens / wollen / gehen

   _____

4. oft / es / nicht / gehen / und / er / rechts / oder / links / schnell / abbiegen / müssen

   _____

5. natürlich / er / in der Sporthalle / abends / auch / trainieren

   _____

| ÜBUNG H | **Fitness Training.** Now it is your turn. Write down five things that you do to keep fit. Use at least one adverb in each sentence. |

_____

_____

_____

_____

_____

4.   Comparative of Adverbs

The comparative form of the adverb is formed by adding -er to the adverb. Often the stem vowel takes an *umlaut*. (See chapter 6.)

Unser Essen hat besser als Eures geschmeckt.   *Our meal tasted better than yours.*

Müssen wir heute früher kommen?   *Do we have to come earlier today?*

ÜBUNG I   **Alles, was du tun kannst, kann ich noch besser!** There's a song with the lyrics: "Anything you can do I can do better." That sums up your friend Woody in a nutshell. Write his reactions to your statements.

EXAMPLE: Ich kann sehr schnell laufen. Aber ich kann schneller laufen.

1. Ich kann meinen Atem sehr lange halten.

   _____

2. Ich kann unheimlich lang schlafen.

   _____

3. Ich muss oft sehr früh aufstehen.

   _____

4. Ich kann schwer arbeiten.

   _____

5. Ich darf bis spät in die Nacht aufbleiben.

   _____

ÜBUNG J   **Ich kann . . .** Now it's your turn again. What do you do better, longer, neater, faster, etc. than your sister? Write 5 comparisons in which you definitely come out the winner. Be nice because soon your sister will have an opportunity to retaliate.

EXAMPLE: Ich kann weiter als meine Schwester springen.

1. tanzen / modern _____

2. schreiben / kreativ _____

3. essen / schnell _____

4. singen / laut _____

5. lernen /intensiv _____

ÜBUNG K   **Der Gegenschlag.** Now it's your sister's turn to rebut your claims. She not only refutes the fact that you aren't better than she. She goes further and uses the expression *nicht mal so . . . wie* (not even as . . . . as) to state that you aren't even as good as she. What are the two sentences she writes for each of your statements?

EXAMPLE: Nein, mein Bruder kann nicht weiter als ich springen.
Er kann nicht mal so weit wie ich springen.

1. _____

_____

2. _____

_____

3. _____

_____

4. _____

_____

5. _____

_____

5.   Superlative of Adverbs

a. The superlative form of the adverb is used to compare the actions of three or more people, places or things. In English we form the superlative either by adding –est to the adverb (fastest) or by using most with the positive form (most intelligently).

b. The German is formed with *am* and *–sten* added to the positive form of the verb. If the adverb required an *umlaut* in the comparative, then it also needs one in the superlative. The chart below shows the positive, comparative and superlative of some common adverbs. As usual, if the adverb ends in *–t, -d, –z* or two consonants followed by an *–n*, then add an *-e-* before the *-sten* to make the word easier to pronounce:

POSITIVE, COMPARATIVE AND SUPERLATIVE OF ADVERBS			
POSITIVE	COMPARATIVE	SUPERLATIVE	ENGLISH
intelligent	intelligenter	am intelligentesten	*intelligent*
klug	klüger	am klügsten	*clever*
kurz	kürzer	am kürzesten	*short*
langsam	langsamer	am langsamsten	*long*
oft	öfter	am öftesten	*often*
schlecht	schlechter	am schlechtesten	*bad, worse, worst*
schnell	schneller	am schnellsten	*fast*
toll	toller	am tollsten	*super, great*

Peter, Alex und Max schwimmen gegeneinander. Max schwimmt am schnellsten.
Peter, Alex and Max are swimming against each other. Max swims fastest.
Wer kann am klügsten arbeiten?   *Who can work most cleverly?*

ÜBUNG L   **Wer rennt schneller?** You have been given the name of three animals and have to rate them.

EXAMPLE: die Maus, der Hase, der Gepard – schnell rennen
        Die Maus rennt schnell. Der Hase rennt schneller. Der Gepard rennt am schnellsten.

1. der Chihuahua, der Dachshund, die Deutsche Dogge – laut bellen

   _____

2. der Storch, der Kranich, der Pfau – herrlich aussehen

   _____

3. die Maus, der Schmetterling, die Biene – klein sein

   _____

4. die Katze, der Bär, das Murmeltier – lang schlafen

   _____

5. der Goldfish, die Forelle, der Haifisch – groß sein

   _____

ÜBUNG M   **Superlative.** You've been reading the book of world records. How would you define the accomplishments of the following record holders?

EXAMPLE: Karten schnell sortieren – Walter Mischmeister
        Walter Mischmeister kann Karten am schnellsten sortieren.

1. amerikanische Quarters lang im Dreh halten– Gloria Umdreher

   _____

2. auf Motorrad weit springen – Egil Knenegel

   _____

3. schnell Schnee schaufeln – Frostina Schneeweiß

   _____

4. laut rülpsen – Raimund Rüpselmacher

   _____

5. fleißig lernen – Salma Studentin

   _____

6. in Schlagsahne tief tauchen – Marianne Weißkopf

   _____

ÜBUNG N   **Deine Umfrage.** Take a survey in your class to find out who participates in which activity and who is the best, fastest, smartest, quickest, etc. Find at least three people for each activity and declare one the best, but use different adverbs to keep it interesting.

EXAMPLE: Peter, Fritz und Marco laufen viel. Marco läuft am langsamsten.

Sandra, Maja und Micky spielen Schach. Maja spielt am tollsten.

_____

_____

_____

_____

_____

_____

6.   Superlative of Adjectives

Unlike adverbs, adjectives take endings. The superlative is formed similarly to the adverb, i.e. *–ste* is still added to the positive form. Regular adjective endings are then added.

POSITIVE, COMPARATIVE AND SUPERLATIVE OF ADJECTIVES			
POSITIVE	COMPARATIVE	SUPERLATIVE	ENGLISH
intelligent	intelligenter	der intelligenteste	*intelligent*
klug	klüger	der klügste	*clever*
kurz	kürzer	der kürzeste	*short*
langsam	langsamer	der langsamste	*long*
schlecht	schlechter	der schlechteste	*bad, worse, worst*
schnell	schneller	der schnellste	*fast*
toll	toller	der tollste	*super, great*

Der beste Fahrer sitzt in dem schnellsten Wagen. *The best driver sits in the fastest car.*

Meine beste Freundin und ich sind in die nächste Stadt gefahren.

My best friend and I drove into the nearest city.

ÜBUNG O | **Die Klassenbesten.** You're creating the page on class superlatives for the school yearbook. You've been given the list of winners. Write them up, being careful to have the correct ending for male, female, or couple.

EXAMPLE: intelligent – Suzy Smartfisch
Suzy Smartfisch ist die Intelligenteste in der Klasse.

1. Marcos Musikliebhaber - musikalisch

_____

2. Lena Lächeltviel – freundlich

_____

3. Eleonore Streberin – erfolgreich

_____

4. Justin Haaresitzengut und Anita Schöngesicht – chic (Paar)

_____

5. Harry Hilfreich – nett

_____

ÜBUNG P | **Die Klassentiere.** Find out who has the biggest, cutest, smartest, etc. pets in your class. Choose at least five different qualities and as many different pets as possible.

EXAMPLE: Jon hat den kürzesten Hund. Andrea hat die schnellste Katze.

1. _____
2. _____
3. _____
4. _____
5. _____

7.   Superlative of Irregular Adverbs and Adverbs

A few adverbs and adjectives do not follow the pattern. It's the same in English. Good things get better. Bad things get worse. There are only six irregular adverbs in German. You will have to memorize them.

POSITIVE, COMPARATIVE AND SUPERLATIVE OF IRREGULAR ADJECTIVES AND ADVERBS			
	COMPARATIVE	SUPERLATIVE	ENGLISH
bald	eher	am ehesten	*soon*
gern	lieber	am liebsten der liebste	*gladly* *the dearest*
groß	größer	am größten der größte	*big, large, tall* *the biggest*
gut	besser	am besten der beste	*good, better, best* *the best*
hoch	höher	am höchsten der höchste	*high* *the highest*
nah	näher	am nächsten der nächste	*near* *the nearest, next*
viel	mehr	am meisten der meiste	*much, more, most* *the most*

Petra hat am meisten Angst vor den Schlangen im Zoo.

Petra is most afraid of the snakes in the zoo.

Vorne ist eine Kletterwand.   Wer kann am höchsten hinaufklettern?

Up ahead is a climbing wall.   Who can climb up the highest?

ÜBUNG Q | **Der Elefant ist am größten.** You've been given a list of three animals and are asked to identify the largest, smallest, fastest, etc.

EXAMPLE: die Biene – die Henne – der Tiger / viel gackern
Die Henne gackert am meisten.

1. die Katze – das Krokodil – der Känguru / hoch springen

   _____

2. der Haifisch – der Schäferhund – das Pferd / schnell schwimmen

   _____

3. der Vogel – die Schlange – der Gorilla / gut singen

   _____

4. die Katze - das Nilpferd - der Schmetterling / viel wiegen

   _____

5. der Esel - die Taube - die Giraffe / fliegt hoch

   _____

6. das Kanninchen- der Büffel - die Ratte / lieb aussehen

   _____

8. viel—viele, wenig—wenige

Note: When to use *viel* and when *viele*? It's easy. *Viel* is an adverb, but also used as an adjective in front of a noun that cannot be counted in units. One has *viel* money, but *viele* coins. Money is not a unit we can count. You can't count three monies. You can count three coins. The English translation for *viel* is "much" and *viele* is "many."

Er hat viel Zeit.   *He has much time (not countable unit).*

Er hat viele Stunden noch.   *He still has many hours (countable units).*

ÜBUNG R | **Viel oder viele?** Woody is back. He always claims to have a lot of things and a lot of money. What would he say in answer to your questions?

EXAMPLE: Hast du Geld? Ich habe viel Geld.
               Hast du Kekse? Ich habe viele Kekse.

1. Hast du Zeit zum Spielen?

    _____

2. Hast du ein Spielzeug?

    _____

3. Hast du ein Auto?

    _____

4. Hast du Freude?

    _____

5. Hast du Freunde?

    _____

The same distinction is made between *wenig* (a little) and *wenige* (a few).

Er hat nur wenig gearbeitet.   *He only worked a little. (adverb)*

Er hat nur wenig Zeit.   *He has only a little time. (not a countable unit)*

Er hat nur wenige Stunden.   *He only has a few hours. (countable units)*

ÜBUNG S | **Wenig oder wenige?** Match the columns. What does Woody have a little of and a few of?

EXAMPLE: Er hat wenige Freunde.

wenig   Freunde
wenige   Geld
              Geduld
              Zeit
              Spielzeuge
              Kuscheltiere

1. _____

2. _____

3. _____

4. _____

5. _____

ÜBUNG T	**Die drei Besten.** Your pen pal and you are comparing what you think about different people. He has asked for the top three in five categories, for example the top three marathon runners in the world or the bottom three chess players. Choose the categories and list the top or bottom three. Truth is not important in this exercise.

EXAMPLE: Dreeve spielt Schach schlecht. Fisher spielt noch schlechter. Brooks spielt am schlechtesten.

_____

_____

_____

_____

_____

_____

_____

_____

_____

_____

_____

CHAPTER 15

Expressing the Future *werden*
Increasing Comparatives

1. Expressing the Future with the Present Tense

In German, the present tense can be paired with an adverb or adverbial phrase to express futurity. Many of the expressions learned in Chapter 14 are used for this purpose.

Wir gehen morgen in die Apotheke und kaufen dir einen Hustensaft.

We will go tomorrow to the pharmacy and buy you some cough syrup.

Some additional adverbs or adverbial expressions you may use to express the future are:

bald	*soon*
gleich	*at once*
morgen	*tomorrow*
übermorgen	*the day after tomorrow*
sofort	*immediately*
später	*later*
am Donnerstag	*on Thursday*
in einer Stunde/Woche	*in an hour/week*
in drei Tagen/Wochen	*in three days/weeks*
in einem Monat/Jahr	*in a month/year*
im Mai	*in May*
nächsten Dienstag	*next Tuesday*
nächste Woche	*next week*
nächsten Monat	*next month*
nächstes Jahr	*next year*

ÜBUNG A | **Die Verhandlungen.** Your mother is complaining and threatening to ground you this weekend. It seems there are several chores that you haven't done yet. Give her a time when you will finish them. Add an element of negotiation to your conversation by adding *Geht das?* Your mother will still let you go to Hendrik's party *am Samstag Abend* if you show you are trying to please her.

EXAMPLE: Ich mähe den Rasen morgen früh. Geht das?

1. Zimmer aufräumen

   _____

2. Wäsche waschen

   _____

3. Schwester mit ihren Hausaufgaben helfen

   _____

4. im Wohnzimmer staubsaugen

   _____

5. Lebensmittel kaufen

   _____

| ÜBUNG B | **Was macht Marta?** Match the columns to express what Marta is going to do.

EXAMPLE: Sie geht heute in die Stadt.

sie →

am Montag   in die Stadt gehen
später   neue Kleider kaufen
heute   ihre Hausaufgaben machen
übermorgen   einen Notebook kaufen
nächsten Monat   Geburtstag haben
morgen   Tennis spielen
in einer Stunde   neue Kleider anprobieren

1. _____
2. _____
3. _____
4. _____
5. _____
6. _____

2. The Verb _werden_

The verb _werden_ is translated as "become." It is irregular and must be memorized.

WERDEN	
SINGULAR	PLURAL
ich werde	wir werden
du wirst	ihr werdet
er, sie, es wird	sie werden
Sie werden	

| ÜBUNG C | **Was willst du werden?** Ask five classmates what they want to become and record their answers. Remember, there is no article used before nationalities and professions. |

EXAMPLE: Donna will Polizistin werden.

1. _____

2. _____

3. _____

4. _____

5. _____

| ÜBUNG D | **Das Wetter bei uns.** Write your pen pal a message telling her how the weather changes in your area. Choose your adjectives from the list below. Don't forget to use some comparative forms. |

kalt, eiskalt, heiß, warm, wärmer, regnerisch, kühl, grau, sonnig, usw.

EXAMPLE: Im Juli wird es heiß.

1. Im September _____

2. Im Januar _____

3. Im Mai _____

4. Im August _____

5. Nächste Woche _____

3.   *immer* with the Comparative

In English, a sentence is emphasized by repeating the comparative, e.g. "The weather is becoming grayer and grayer." In German the comparative is not used twice, it is combined with the word *immer. Das Wetter wird immer grauer.* This construction is often, but not always, used with the verb *werden.*

Der olympische Sportler schwimmt immer schneller.

The Olympic athlete is swimming faster and faster.

Diese Stadt wird immer teuerer.   *This city is becoming more and more expensive.*

| ÜBUNG E | **Wieder Ärger mit der Mutter.** Your mother is still annoyed and complaining about your habits. You are getting worse and worse, your music is louder and louder every day, etc. Write three negative things she might say about you. Answer them with three positive statements about your behavior. |

EXAMPLE: MUTTER: Du wirst immer schlampiger. (schlampig = *sloppy*)
You are getting sloppier and sloppier.
DU: Aber ich nehme jetzt immer mehr Zeit mit meinen Haaren.
But I'm taking more and more time with my hair now.

1. MUTTER: _____
  DU: _____

2. MUTTER: _____
  Du: _____

3. Mutter: _____
  Du: _____

4.   The Future Tense

German also has a formal future tense. The auxiliary verb *werden*, now translated into English as "will," becomes the finite verb. It's in the second element and an infinitive completer goes to the end of the sentence.

Er wird uns morgen besuchen.	*He will visit us tomorrow.*
Meine zwei Brüder werden Lehrer werden.	*My two brothers will become teachers.*
Werdet ihr Brot beim Bäcker kaufen?	*Will you buy bread at the baker's?*

ÜBUNG F   **Die Zukunftspläne.** Make a list of the things you think you and your friends and family might do sometime in the future.

EXAMPLE: Markus wird nach Deutschland fahren.

1. Mein Vater / Urlaub haben

_____

2. Meine Mutter / neuen Job anfangen

_____

3. Mein Bruder und meine Schwester / Fahrschule machen

_____

4. Meine beste Freundin / Geburtstag haben

_____

5. Ihr, Gerda und Gerlinde, uns besuchen

_____

ÜBUNG G   **Und du?** What will your life be like in 20 years? Make 5 predictions.

EXAMPLE: In 20 Jahren werde ich einen Mann, ein großes Haus und drei Kinder haben.

1. _____

2. _____

3. _____

4. _____

5. _____

5.   The Word Order of the Future Tense

a. The Future Tense in a Subordinate Clause

The rules for word order don't change if the future tense is in a subordinate clause. The clause is introduced by the subordinate conjunction, and the finite form of the verb (which is *werden*), goes to the end of the clause.

Ich hoffe, dass Sie uns bald besuchen werden.   *I hope that you will visit us soon.*

Wisst ihr, wann ihr Tennis spielen werdet?   *Do you know when you will play tennis?*

ÜBUNG H **Was werden wir tun?** You and your friend are discussing the upcoming class trip. You have some questions for your friend. Use the formal future tense to ask your questions.

EXAMPLE: Weisst du, (ob) wir / am Mittwoch / spät / ankommen
Weißt du, ob wir am Mittwoch spät ankommen werden?

1. Weißt du, (ob) Herr Marzipan / wir / am Flughafen / abholen

_____

2. Kannst du mir schreiben, (wie) wir / vom Flughafen / in die Stadt / fahren

_____

3. Weißt du, (wie viele) / eigentlich / nach Österreich / mitfahren

_____

4. Ich möchte wissen, (wann) wir / nach Salzburg / fahren

_____

5. Weiß Herr Marzipan, (dass) ich / während / die Reise / Geburtstag / haben

_____

ÜBUNG I **Am Wochenende.** Your teacher tells you what he hopes you will do over the weekend.

EXAMPLE: Ich hoffe. (dass) ihr / viel / lernen   Ich hoffe, dass ihr viel lernen werdet.

1. dass / ihr / die Hausaufgaben / machen

   _____

2. dass / ihr / gut/ sich benehmen

   _____

3. dass / Marcos / das Schachturnier / gewinnen

   _____

4. dass / Vera / viel Erfolg / bei dem Schiwettbewerb / haben

   _____

5. dass / Albert und Allen / gut / in Berlin / ankommen

   _____

b. The Future Tense with a Modal Verb

The VIM (verb-infinitive-modal) word order remains the same with a future tense.

Ich werde ihn nicht sehen können. *I will not be able to see him.*
    verb   infinitive modal

Wirst du uns nächste Woche besuchen können? *Will you be able to visit us next*
    verb   infinitive   modal   *week?*

ÜBUNG J   **Verschiedene Möglichkeiten?** You ask Herr Marzipan about various possibilities during your upcoming trip. Write down his answers so that you can show them to other students.

EXAMPLE: Bier trinken? Ihr werdet kein Bier trinken dürfen.

1. in die Disco gehen?

   _____

2. bis spät in die Nacht in der Stadt bleiben?

   _____

3. in einem guten Restaurant essen?

   _____

4. alleine überall hingehen?

   _____

5. Auto fahren?

   _____

ÜBUNG K   **Deine Wunschliste.** Write your own list of things you hope you will be able to do on your next trip.

EXAMPLE: Ich hoffe, dass ich viele neue Erlebnisse haben werde.

1. _____
2. _____
3. _____
4. _____
5. _____

| ÜBUNG L | **Jetzt darf ich!** When you turn 18 there will be many things that you will be allowed to do as an adult. List at least five of them.

EXAMPLE: Wenn ich endlich 18 Jahre alt bin, werde ich wählen dürfen.

_____

_____

_____

_____

_____

| ÜBUNG M | **Zukunftsvorstellungen.** You've described what you think your life will be like in 20 years. Choose 3 friends or classmates and write predictions of what their lives will be like. Include at least three observations for each person.

1. Nummer eins heißt _____.

_____

_____

_____

_____

2. Nummer zwei heißt _____.

_____

_____

_____

_____

_____

3. Nummer drei heißt _____.

_____

_____

_____

_____

CHAPTER 16
Past Tense

1. The Simple Past Tense of *sein*

Sein is the infinitive of the verb "to be". The present tense translates as "am," "is" or "are." The past tense translates as "was" or "were."

THE SIMPLE PAST OF **SEIN — WAREN**			
SINGULAR		PLURAL	
ich war	*I was*	**wir war –en**	*we were*
du war – st	*you (informal) were*	**ihr war–t**	*you (informal) were*
er, sie, es war	*he, she, or it was*	**sie war –en**	*they were*
Sie war – en	*You (formal) were*		

ÜBUNG A | **Wo warst du gestern?** Most of the class was in the city yesterday. Write a list of where everyone was.

EXAMPLE: Heiko und Benno waren in der Sporthalle.

Jan	in der Sporthalle
Sie, Frau Penthes	bei der Bank
Heiko und Benno	im Museum
Krista sein	im Kino
Du, Beate	in der Bibliothek
Herr Marzipan	in der Schwimmhalle
Ihr, Richard und Micki	in der Sporthalle

1. _____

2. _____

3. _____

4. _____

5. _____

6. _____

ÜBUNG B **Fragen.** You hear one side of a conversation. Fill in the possible questions.

EXAMPLE: Wo wart ihr? Wir waren in der Sporthalle.

1. _____

Marika war auch da.

2. _____

Wir waren auch im Schwimmbad.

3. _____

Ich war nicht sehr lange dort.

4. _____

Lena war nur zehn Minuten da.

5. _____

Ja, er war auch im Schwimmbad.

2.   The Simple Past Tense of *haben*

Haben is the infinitive form of the verb "to have." Its past tense translates as "had."

THE SIMPLE PAST TENSE OF **HABEN – HATTEN**			
SINGULAR		PLURAL	
ich hatte	*I had*	**wir hatt –en**	*we had*
du hatt – est	*you (informal) had*	**ihr hatt – et**	*you (informal) had*
er, sie, es hatt – e	*he, she, or it had*	**sie hatt –en**	*they had*
Sie hatt – en	*You (formal) had*		

ÜBUNG C	**Inhalt der Rucksäcke.** After your recent hiking trip Mathias asks you what kind of interesting things different people had in their rucksacks.

EXAMPLE: Mika; Was hatte Mika in ihrem Rucksack?
ein CD-Spieler; Sie hatte einen CD-Spieler.

1. Herr Marzipan _____

   das Klassenbuch _____

2. Markus _____

   viele Süssigkeiten _____

3. du _____

   mein Teddybär _____

4. Mario und Maria _____

   ihre Deutschbücher _____

5. Frau Raetzel _____

   ihre *Schminke _____

*also called **das Make-up** in German

3.   The Simple Past Tense of Weak (Regular) Verbs

The simple past tense, often called the narrative past, is used to discuss events that have already happened. It translates into English as "played," "did play" or "was playing." This tense is usually reserved for written stories or when relating a sequence of events. A single event in the past is still expressed by the present perfect.

Rottkäppchen <u>packte</u> den Kuchen in ihren Korb <u>ein, sagte</u> ihrer Mutter „Auf Wiedersehen" und <u>spazierte</u> durch den Wald auf dem Weg zu ihrer Grossmutter. Unterwegs <u>pflückte</u> sie ihr einige Blumen und <u>steckte</u> sie auch in ihren Korb.

Little Red Riding Hood <u>packed</u> the cake into her basket, <u>said</u> "goodbye" to her mother and <u>walked</u> through the woods on the way to her grandmother's. Along the way she <u>picked</u> a few flowers for her and <u>put</u> them into her basket also.

a. Formation of the Simple Past Tense

There is no change in word order from the present tense. The simple past tense is formed by adding the endings from the chart on the following page to the verb stem.

SIMPLE PAST TENSE OF WEAK (REGULAR) VERBS	
SINGULAR	PLURAL
ich spiel – te *I played, I did play, I was playing*	**wir spiel – ten** *we played, we did play, we were playing*
du spiel – test *you (informal) played, did play, were playing*	**ihr spiel – tet** *you (informal) played, did play, were playing*
er, sie, es spiel – te *he, she, or it played, did play, was playing*	**sie spiel – ten** *they played, they did play, they were playing*
Sie spiel – ten *You (formal) played, did play, were playing*	

NOTE: If the stem ends in *–t, –d,* or two consonants followed by an *–n,* add *–e* before the *–te* ending to facilitate pronunciation.

> **Er arbeitete in der Schule. (arbeiten)**   *He worked in the school.*
>
> **Die neue Stadtsgallerie öffnete letzte Woche. (öffnen)**
>
> *The new City Gallery opened last week.*

ÜBUNG D   **Eine Geschichte erzählen.** In preparation for a creative writing assignment, you've been given some pictures with suggested verbs. Create a story. Like all good German fairy tales, the story starts with *Eines Tages* and suggests at the end that they are living happily ever after.

spazieren

weinen

eine Stunde warten

Blumen pflücken

eine Decke ausbreiten
Picknickkorb aufmachen

Mittagsschläfchen
machen / stricken

Eines Tages _____

_____

_____

_____

_____

_____

_____

_____

_____

_____ . Und dort sitzen sie noch bis heute glücklich im Sonnenschein.

ÜBUNG E | **Hoppla!** Whoops. Helga finished her story. It's good. She even added in a wolf. Only problem is, she forgot it was supposed to be in the past tense. Can you help her change it quickly before you must hand them in? There are only 20 verbs to change.

Felix und seine Schwester Lena ~~spazieren~~ am Montag durch den Wald. She wollen ihre
                                  spazierten

Großmutter besuchen. Lena hat Brot und Kuchen in ihrem Korb. Leider hat Felix aber jetzt

Hunger. Er weint. Lena zeigt auf ihre Uhr. Es ist erst 11 Uhr. Die Kinder warten bis zwölf,

dann packt Lena den Picknickkorb aus. Sie merken einen Wolf. Der Wolf schaut auf ihr

Essen auf. Lena und Felix haben Angst, aber sie teilen ihr Brot und ihren Kuchen mit dem

Wolf. Der Wolf dankt ihnen. Er muss dann weggehen und *seine* Oma besuchen. Er sagt „Auf

Wiedersehen". Die Kinder machen noch eine Stunde Pause. Felix macht ein kleines

Mittagsschläfchen und Lena strickt. Und dort sind sie noch heute glücklich in der Sonne.

4.   The Simple Past Tense of Stem Vowel Change Verbs

Certain verbs change the vowel from the present to the past tense. Most are already familiar from English, e.g. "drink" "becomes drank" in the past; "go," "went;" and "give," "gave." Just as in English, these vowel changes will have to be memorized.

There are four vowel change combinations that form the past tense of almost all strong verbs. Following is a list of many of the strong verbs with their past tense. Notice that in the past tense neither the *ich* nor the *er/sie/es* form takes any ending.

1. Verbs with Stem Vowel Change to *A* in the Past Tense

SIMPLE PAST TENSE OF VERBS WITH **A**-VOWEL CHANGE	
SINGULAR	PLURAL
ich gab *I gave, I did give, I was giving*	**wir gab – en** *we gave, did give, were giving*
***du gab – st** *you (informal) gave, did give, were giving*	**ihr gab– t** *you (informal) gave, did give, were giving*
er, sie, es gab *he, she, or it gave, did give, was giving*	**sie gab – en** *they gave, did give, were giving*
Sie gab – en *you (formal) gave, did give, were giving*	

*if the *du*-form already ends in –s or –ß, then add only a –t

beginnen	**begann**	*begin, began*
bekommen	**bekam**	*receive, received*
brechen	**brach**	*break, broke*
essen	**aß**	*eat, ate*
finden	**fand**	*find, found*
geben	**gab**	*give, gave*
geschehen	**geschah**	*happen, happened*
helfen	**half**	*help, helped*
kommen	**kam**	*come, came*
lesen	**las**	*read, read*
nehmen	**nahm**	*take, took*
sehen	**sah**	*see, saw*
sitzen	**sass**	*sit, sat*
sprechen	**sprach**	*speak, spoke*
stehen	**stand**	*stand, stood*
trinken	**trank**	*drink, drank*
tun	**tat**	*do, did*
vergessen	**vergass**	*forget, forgot*

ÜBUNG F   **Im Restaurant.** Marika is talking about her visit to a German restaurant last Saturday. Because she is relating a series of events, her verbs are in the simple past. What does she say?

EXAMPLE: ich / ein gutes Restaurant / in der Stadt / finden
Ich fand ein gutes Restaurant in der Stadt.

1. meine Oma / ihre Brille / vergessen // ich / also / die Speisekarte / vorlesen

   _____

2. was / geschehen?

   _____

3. wir / eine Wurstplatte / bekommen

   _____

4. Und / wir / eine Apfelschorle / trinken

   _____

5. wir / sehr langsam / essen / und / über vieles / sprechen

   _____

6. wir / die Wurstplatte / sehr gut / finden

   _____

| ÜBUNG G | **Dein Samstag.** Now it's your turn to tell Marika what you did on Saturday. Write at least 6 sentences using at least five of the verbs from the list on page 163. |

_____

_____

_____

_____

_____

2. Verbs with Stem Vowel Changes to _IE_ in the Past Tense

SIMPLE PAST TENSE OF VERBS WITH **IE**-VOWEL CHANGE	
SINGULAR	PLURAL
ich schrieb _I wrote, I did write, I was writing_	**wir schrieb – en** _we wrote, did write, were writing_
*du schrieb – st _you (informal) wrote, did write, were writing_	**ihr schrieb– t** _you (informal) wrote, did write, were writing_
er, sie, es schrieb _he, she, or it wrote, did write, was writing_	**sie schrieb – en** _they wrote, did write, were writing_
Sie schrieb – en _you (formal) wrote, did write, were writing_	

*if the _du_-form already ends in –s or –ß, then add only a –t

bleiben	blieb	*stay, stayed*
fallen	fiel	*fall, fell*
heißen	hieß	*be called, was called*
laufen	lief	*walk or run, walked or ran*
schreiben	schrieb	*write, wrote*
steigen	stieg	*to climb*

ÜBUNG H   **Marikas Sommer.** Marika wrote you a story about her summer. The paper was torn apart by your younger brother. Match the columns to re-construct the story. Add time adverbs like *dann, später*, etc.

EXAMPLE: Ich lief in den Wald.

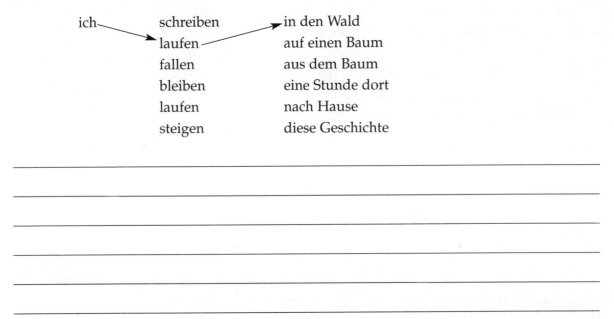

ich → schreiben → in den Wald
laufen → auf einen Baum
fallen   aus dem Baum
bleiben   eine Stunde dort
laufen   nach Hause
steigen   diese Geschichte

_____

_____

_____

_____

_____

_____

3. Verbs with Vowel Changes to *U* in the Past Tense

| SIMPLE PAST TENSE OF VERBS WITH **U**-VOWEL CHANGE | |
SINGULAR	PLURAL
ich trug *I wore, I did wear, I was wearing*	**wir trug – en** *we wore, did wear, were wearing*
*du trugs – st *you (informal) wore, did wear, were wearing*	**ihr trug– t** *you (informal) wore, did wear, were wearing*
er, sie, es trug *he, she, or it wore, did wear, was wearing*	**sie trug – en** *they wore, did wear, were wearing*
Sie trug – en *you (formal) wore, did wear, were wearing*	

*if the *du*-form already ends in –*s* or –*ß*, then add only a –*t*

einladen	lud ein	*invite, invited*
fahren	fuhr	*drive or ride drove or rode*
tragen	trug	*carry or wear, carried or wore*
wachsen	wuchs	*grow*
waschen	wusch	*wash, washed*
wissen	wusste	*know, knew*

ÜBUNG I | **Eine Einladung.** Diana tells the story of a special dinner.

EXAMPLE: am Samstag / Darien / ich / zum Essen / einladen
Am Samstag lud Darien mich zum Essen ein.

1. ich / er / eine Antwort / schreiben

_____

2. dann / am Montag / ich / zu ihm / fahren

_____

3. ich / schon / wissen / wo / er / wohnen

_____

4. ich /mein / blau / Kleid / tragen

_____

5. wir / die Hände / zusammen / waschen

_____

6. eine Gurke / auf den Boden / fallen

_____

7. sie / da / bleiben / bis / sein / klein / Bruder / kam

_____

8. wir / um sieben / essen / und / bis / zehn Uhr / am Tisch / sitzen / und / sprechen

_____

9. der / Abend / schön / sein

_____

4. Verbs with Stem Vowel Changes to *I* in the Past Tense

SIMPLE PAST TENSE OF VERBS WITH I-VOWEL CHANGE	
SINGULAR	PLURAL
ich ging *I went, I did go, I was going* - en	**wir ging – en** *we went, did go, were going*
*du ging – st *you (informal) went, did go, were going*	**ihr ging– t** *you (informal) went, did go, were going*
er, sie, es ging *he, she, or it went, did go, was going*	**sie ging – en** *they went, did go, were going*
Sie ging – en *you (formal) went, did go, were going*	

*if the *du*-form already ends in –*s* or –*ß*, then add only a –*t*

anfangen	fing an	*begin*
beißen	biss	*bite*
fangen	fing	*catch*
gehen	ging	*go*
pfeifen	pfiff	*whistle*
reiten	ritt	*ride, rode (an animal)*

ÜBUNG J | **Eine komische Tiergeschichte.** A strange animal story. Use the pictures and each of the verbs in the list above at least once to tell the story of the bizarre incidents that happened one night at the circus. Write this story in the narrative past.

EXAMPLE: Der Löwe fing ein Kartenspiel an.

_____

_____

_____

_____

_____

_____

_____

_____

_____

5. Verbs with Vowel Changes to *O* in the Past Tense

SIMPLE PAST TENSE OF VERBS WITH **O**-VOWEL CHANGE	
SINGULAR	PLURAL
ich flog *I flew, I did fly, I was flying*	**wir flog – en** *we flew, did fly, were flying*
*du flog – st *you (informal) flew, did fly, were flying*	**ihr flog– t** *you (informal) flew, did fly, were flying*
er, sie, es flog *he, she, or it flew, did fly, was flying they*	**sie flog – en** *flew, did fly, were flying*
Sie flog – en *you (formal) flew, did fly, were flying*	

*if the *du*-form already ends in *–s* or *–ß*, then add only a *–t*

biegen	**bog**	*bend, bended*
fliegen	**flog**	*fly, flew*
genießen	**genoss**	*enjoy*
kriechen	**kroch**	*crawl, creep*
riechen	**roch**	*smell*
verlieren	**verlor**	*lose*

ÜBUNG K	**Ein Tag im Leben von Suzy Schildkröte**. Suzy Schildkröte had a bad day yesterday. What do you think happened? Using all the verbs above in the simple past tense, tell her story.

_____

_____

_____

_____

_____

_____

_____

_____

_____

ÜBUNG L	**Leonies Tag.** After Suzy's crazy day, Leonie's seems so calm. Use the pictures to write a story about Leonie and what happened to her.

EXAMPLE: Leonie fuhr in die Stadt.

1. _____

2. _____

3. Und dann_____

4. _____

5. _____

6. _____

| ÜBUNG M | **Der Wettbewerb.** You decide to enter a short story contest. Write your entry using the narrative past tense. Use as many of the verbs from the lists as you can. Use adverbs to keep the story flow. Remember all the things you can do to vary your writing and add interest, i.e. use sentences with more than one clause and vary the word order. |

_____

_____

_____

_____

_____

_____

_____

_____

_____

_____

CHAPTER 17
Verbs – Comprehensive Review

By now four tenses and all four principle parts of the verb have been discussed. There are still two more tenses and two voices of the verb to be discussed. This chapter will serve as a review and consolidated study guide before proceeding.

1. Tenses of the Verb

German verbs have six tenses. The four presented this far in the series are: the present, the past, the future and the present perfect.

a. Present tense

The present tense of the verb has three direct translations:

I buy, I am buying and *I do buy*.

It is formed by adding personal endings to the stem of the verb.

| ÜBUNG A | **Präsens.** Fill in the table below with the verb *kaufen*. |

PRESENT TENSE CONJUGATION OF REGULAR VERBS	
SINGULAR	PLURAL
ich	wir
du	ihr
er, sie, es	sie
Sie	

Strong verbs change the vowel in the *du-* and the *er/sie/es* forms only. There are three patterns of vowel changes.

a becomes *ä*   *tragen*
e becomes *i*   *helfen*
e becomes *ie* *lesen*

| ÜBUNG B | **Präsens mit Vokaländerung.** Fill in the table on top of page 172 with the present tense stem-change verbs in German. |

PRESENT TENSE CONJUGATION OF VERBS WITH STEM-VOWEL CHANGE							
SINGULAR				PLURAL			
	tragen	helfen	lesen		tragen	helfen	lesen
ich				wir			
du				ihr			
er, sie, es				sie			
Sie				Sie			

ÜBUNG C **Verbenliste im Präsens.** In the following table write as many verbs in each category as possible. You may add to this list as you learn more to create a more complete reference for yourself.

a ⟶⟶	ä	e	i	e	ie
fahren	fährt				

b. Past Tense (Simple Past, Narrative Past, Imperfect Tense)

The past tense of the verb, also referred to as the simple past, the imperfect or the narrative past, is used when telling a story or reciting a series of events. The simple past is used more often in writing than in speaking. It has three direct translations:

I bought, I did buy and *I was buying*

ÜBUNG D **Vergangenheit.** Fill in the table on top of page 173 with the verb *kaufen*, this time in the simple past tense. It is formed by adding *–te* to the stem of the verb, and then adding personal endings. The *ich-* and the *er/sie/es* forms take no additional endings in the simple past tense.

PRESENT TENSE CONJUGATION OF REGULAR VERBS	
SINGULAR	PLURAL
ich	wir
du	ihr
er, sie, es	sie
Sie	

NOTE: Many strong verbs change their vowel between the present and the simple past. There are five basic patterns of vowel changes. There are no personal endings on the *ich-* and the *er/sie/es* forms of vowel change verbs in the simple past tense.

e, i or *o*	becomes *a*	*geben, gab*
		finden, fand
		kommen, kam
a, au, or *ei*	becomes *ie*	*fallen, fiel*
		laufen, lief
		bleiben, blieb
a or *i*	becomes *u*	*tragen, trug*
		wissen, wusste
a, e, or *ei*	becomes *i*	*anfangen, fing an*
		gehen, ging
		pfeifen, pfiff
ie	becomes *o*	*einbiegen, bog ein*

The following table illustrates three of the five past tense stem-vowel change patterns.

ÜBUNG E	**Vergangenheitsformen.** Fill it in using either *tragen, gehen, fliegen, helfen,* or *schreiben*.

PAST TENSE CONJUGATION OF VERBS WITH **A-**, **IE-** AND **U** STEM-VOWEL CHANGES							
SINGULAR				PLURAL			
	A-past tense	IE-past tense	U-past tense		A-past tense	IE- past tense	U-past tense
ich				wir			
du				ihr			
er, sie, es				sie			
Sie				Sie			

ÜBUNG F   **Verbenliste in der Vergangenheit.** In the following table write as many verbs in each of the above categories as possible. You may add to this list as you learn more to create a more complete reference for yourself.

VERBS WITH **A-**, **IE-** AND **U** PAST TENSE STEM-VOWEL CHANGES		
A-past tense	**IE-past tense**	**U-past tense**

The following table illustrates the last two of five past tense stem-vowel change patterns.

ÜBUNG G   **Vergangenheit II.** Fill it in using either *gehen, anfangen, fliegen,* or *kriechen.*

PAST TENSE CONJUGATION OF VERBS WITH **I** AND **O** STEM-VOWEL CHANGES					
SINGULAR			PLURAL		
	I-past tense	**O-past tense**		**I-past tense**	**O-past tense**
ich			wir		
du			ihr		
er, sie, es			sie		
Sie			Sie		

ÜBUNG H	**Vergangenheitsverbenliste II.** In the following table write as many verbs in each category as possible. You may add to this list as you learn more to create a more complete reference for yourself.

PAST TENSE CONJUGATION OF VERBS WITH **I** AND **O** STEM-VOWEL CHANGES			
I-past tense		**O**-past tense	

c. Future Tense

The future tense has two translations:

I will buy and *I am going to buy*

It is formed using the present tense of the auxiliary verb *werden* as the finite verb (the part of the verb that takes personal endings) and an infinitive completer at the end of the clause or sentence. Because the verb is used only as an infinitive completer, there is no difference in the conjugation of weak and strong verbs.

ÜBUNG I	**Die Zukunft.** Fill in the following table using the verb *kaufen*. Include the auxiliary verb in the table.

FUTURE TENSE CONJUGATION OF VERBS	
SINGULAR	PLURAL
ich	wir
du	ihr
er, sie, es	sie
Sie	

d. Present Perfect Tense (Conversational Past, Perfect)

2.   When to Use the Present Perfect Tense

The present perfect tense, also referred to as the perfect or the conversational past, is used to express an isolated instance in the past (as opposed to a series of occurrences in the past).

Both the simple past and the present perfect express past actions. When is the present perfect used and when the past? The present perfect tense is like a snapshot. It captures one moment. The narrative past is more like a film that captures a series of moments. When your narrative contains a series of verbs, then the simple past is preferred.

There is only one instance when there is no choice about which tense to use. If the verb expresses "was ...ing" (e.g., "I was going,") the simple past must be used.

Ich kaufte eben einen neuen Regenmantel, als sie mich sah.

I was just buying a new raincoat, when she saw me.

In almost all other cases, the choice between simple past and the present perfect is dependent upon whether one is narrating a series of actions (simple past), or just one isolated incident in the past (present perfect).

3.   Formation of the Present Perfect Tense

The present perfect tense is formed using the present tense of *haben* or *sein* as an auxiliary verb followed by the past participle (the *ge*-form) of the verb at the end of its clause or sentence. If the verb shows motion towards a goal, state of being or a change of state, *sein* is the auxiliary verb. All other verbs use *haben* as their auxiliary verb. *Sein* verbs can never take a direct object. If a sentence has a direct object, then the auxiliary verb will be *haben*.

There are a few verbs that can take either *haben* or *sein* depending upon its use in the sentence. In the sentence below there is motion towards a goal (driving to the hospital), but no direct object. The auxiliary verb is *sein*.

Er ist mit meinem Vater ins Krankenhaus gefahren.

He drove with my father to the hospital.

In the next sentence he is still driving to the hospital, but this time there is a direct object. "He is driving my father to the hospital." Because of the direct object, *fahren* now takes *haben* as an auxiliary verb.

Er hat meinen Vater ins Krankenhaus gefahren.

He drove my father to the hospital.

The present perfect tense is translated as:

I bought, I did buy, I have bought

ÜBUNG J | **Perfekt.** Fill in the chart with the present perfect tense of *kaufen*. Include the auxiliary verb.

PRESENT PERFECT TENSE CONJUGATION OF WEAK VERBS	
SINGULAR	PLURAL
ich	wir
du	ihr
er, sie, es	sie
Sie	

Strong verbs show a vowel change in the past participle. (See table page 198).

ÜBUNG K | **Perfektsformen.** Fill in the table below in the present perfect tense with one strong verb that takes *haben* as a helping verb, and one that takes *sein*. Use *tragen* and *schwimmen*. Include the helping verb for each.

PRESENT PERFECT TENSE CONJUGATION OF STEM-VOWEL VERBS					
SINGULAR			PLURAL		
	tragen	schwimmen		tragen	schwimmen
ich			wir		
du			ihr		
er, sie, es			sie		
Sie			Sie		

4.   The Principle Parts of Verbs

All students learning English memorize the principle parts of verbs, even native-speakers:

eat, ate, eaten   begin, began, begun   drive, drove, driven   see, saw, seen

German also has principle parts which need memorizing. Various stem vowel changes have been presented in this book. This chapter is an opportunity to pull all that information together into a single, comprehensive reference section.

Most important are the auxiliary verbs *haben*, *sein* and *werden*. All three are irregular. They are the building blocks that help form all six German tenses.

ÜBUNG L **Hilfsverben.** Fill in the table below. If you need help, use a dictionary or access an online dictionary.

PRINCIPAL PARTS OF HELPING VERBS				
INFINITIVE	3RD PERSON SINGULAR PRESENT TENSE	3RD PERSON SINGULAR SIMPLE PAST TENSE	3RD PERSON SINGULAR PRESENT PERFECT TENSE	ENGLISH MEANING
	hat		hat gehabt	
		war		to be
werden		wurde	ist geworden	

ÜBUNG M **Modalverben.** All the modal verbs follow a specific pattern. Fill in the chart from your notes.

PRINCIPAL PARTS OF MODAL VERBS				
INFINITIVE	3RD PERSON SINGULAR PRESENT TENSE	3RD PERSON SINGULAR SIMPLE PAST TENSE	3RD PERSON SINGULAR PRESENT PERFECT TENSE	ENGLISH MEANING
	darf			
können				
			hat gemocht	
müssen				
				should
		wollte		

ÜBUNG N **Starke Verben.** German stem vowel changes usually follow seven basic patterns. They will become apparent to you as you fill in the following table. It contains many of the most frequently used German verbs. If you do not remember them, use a dictionary or access an online dictionary to help you fill it in.

PRINCIPAL PARTS OF COMMONLY USED STRONG VERBS				
INFINITIVE	3RD PERSON SINGULAR PRESENT TENSE	3RD PERSON SINGULAR SIMPLE PAST TENSE	3RD PERSON SINGULAR PRESENT PERFECT TENSE	ENGLISH MEANING
anfangen				
			hat angerufen	
		begann		
	zieht an			
				stay, remain
		bog		
brechen				
	bringt			

	PRINCIPAL PARTS OF COMMONLY USED STRONG VERBS (continued)			
INFINITIVE	3RD PERSON SINGULAR PRESENT TENSE	3RD PERSON SINGULAR SIMPLE PAST TENSE	3RD PERSON SINGULAR PRESENT PERFECT TENSE	ENGLISH MEANING
			hat eingeladen	
				eat
	fährt			
fallen				
		fing		
	gefällt			
			hat gefunden	
				fly
	gibt			
geschehen				happen
	hält			
			hat geheißen	
		half		
			ist gekommen	
	läuft			
lesen				
				take
		ritt		
rufen				
	schläft			
		schlug		
schließen				
				cut
				write
	schwimmt			
			hat gesehen	
singen				
		saß		
	spricht			
				stand
sterben				
tragen				
				drink
	tut			
			hat vergessen	
waschen				
werfen				
		zog		

That's it! You now have many more tools that you can use to make your German varied and interesting. Experiment with different tenses until you are comfortable using these four.

| ÜBUNG O | **Mein Märchen.** You have an assignment for German that sounds like a lot of fun. You have been asked to write an original fairy tale. There are no guidelines other than the fact that it must be appealing to a third or fourth grader. Write your narrative in the simple past, but include direct quotes from your characters that allow you to use the present, perfect and future tenses also. Your story must be at least ten sentences long. Three of those sentences should contain more than one clause. |

Es gab einmal . . . . _____

_____

_____

_____

_____

_____

_____

_____

_____

_____

_____

_____

_____

_____

_____

_____ . . . Und wenn sie nicht gestorben sind, dann leben sie noch heute.

CHAPTER 18
Special Use Verbs

1. *hin-* and *her-*

Wo gehst du hin? and *Wo kommst du her?* are familiar to all learners. The separable prefixes *hin-* and *her-* may be attached to almost any verb of motion. They signal movement. *Hin-* is used if the movement is away from the speaker and *her-* if the movement is toward the speaker.

Komm her! *Come here.* **Jetzt lauf zu deiner Mutter hin!** *Now walk to your mother.*

The two separable prefixes are often attached to prepositions forming a longer separable prefix that indicates the direction of the movement.

Ich bin hier oben. Steig herauf! *I'm up here. Climb up.*
Er steigt auf den Berg hinauf. *He's climbing up the mountain.*

| ÜBUNG A | **Was sagen die Leute?** What are the people saying? |

EXAMPLE: Geh hinaus!

1. _____

2. _____

3. _____

4. _____

5. _____

2. *legen* and *liegen*

Many English-speakers have difficulties distinguishing the verbs "lay" and "lie" in their own language. This causes confusion between *legen* (to lay) and *liegen* (to lie) in German.

Legen (lay) must have a direct object.

Leg das Buch auf den Tisch!	*Lay the book on the table.*
Leg dich hin.	**Lay (yourself) down.*

*English does not use the reflexive object. Therefore "lie down" is correct in English.

Liegen cannot have a direct object.

Ich liege hier gemütlich in der Sonne.	*I'm lying here in the sun.*
Das Buch liegt auf dem Tisch.	*The book is lying on the table.*

ÜBUNG B   **Liege ich oder lege ich?** Use *liegen* or *legen* to
express what is happening in the pictures.

EXAMPLE: Er legt das Buch auf den Tisch.

1. _____

2. _____

3. _____

4. _____

5. _____

3.   *setzen* and *sitzen*

Setzen (set) and *sitzen* (sit) are similar to *liegen* and *legen*.

Setzen must have a direct object.

Setz dich!	*Sit (yourself) down!*
Ich habe die Tasse auf den Tisch gesetzt.	*I set the cup on the table.*

Sitzen cannot take a direct object.

Deine Schwester sitzt vor dem Fernseher.	*Your sister is sitting in front of the TV.*
Wo sitzt du im Chor?	*Where do you sit in the choir?*

| ÜBUNG C | **Was passiert?** Express what is going on in the pictures.

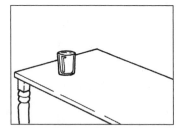

EXAMPLE: Die Tasse sitzt auf dem Tisch.

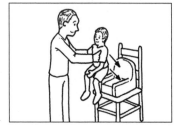

1. _____

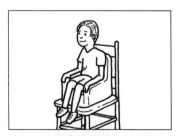

2. _____

3. _____

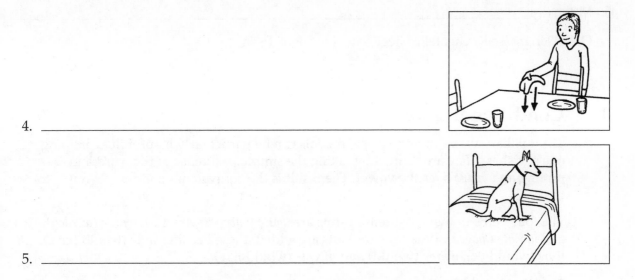

4. _____

5. _____

NOTE: The motion of setting, laying, or standing something down somewhere is considered motion towards a goal. The prepositional phrase answering the question "where (to)" therefore takes the accusative case.

> **Ich lege die CDs in den Spieler ein.**   *I'm laying the CDs into the player.*

The verbs of sitting, lying or standing in one position require no motion towards a goal. The prepositional phrase answering the question "where" must now take a dative object.

> **Die CDs liegen schon in dem Spieler.**   *The CDs are already (lying) in the player.*

ÜBUNG D   **Tisch decken!** You and your classmate are writing a skit about parents and children. For one part you write a dialog in which your mother tells you to set the table. Fill in her commands and answer that the items are on the table already.

EXAMPLE: Lege die Tischdecke auf den Tisch. Sie liegt schon auf dem Tisch.

1. MUTTI – _____

   DU – Das Besteck liegt auch schon auf dem Tisch.

   _____

2. MUTTI – Setzt doch die Tassen und Untertassen auf den Tisch.

   _____

   DU – _____

3. MUTTI - Lege doch die neuen Kuchenteller dazu!

   _____

   DU – _____

4. MUTTI - Kannst du auch die blauen Servietten neben die Teller legen?

   DU – _____

5. Mutti – _____

Du – Der grosse Kuchenteller liegt schon auf dem Tisch.

4. Conditional Verbs

The auxiliary verbs **and one of** the modals can be particularly helpful in expressing one's wishes. They are formed by taking the simple past tense of the word and putting an *umlaut* over the vowel. The result is the equivalent of adding "would" to the verb.

The four verbs in their past tense forms are: *hatte (haben)*, *war (sein)*, *wurde (werden)*, and *mochte (mögen)*. When the umlauts are added, these become *hätte* (would have), *wäre* (would be), *würde* (would) and *möchte* (would like).

a. *hätte* – would have

The verb *hätte* is used often with gern to mean "would like" (literally, I would gladly have)

Ich hätte gern eine Tasse Kaffee.   *I would like a cup of coffee*

HÄTTEN			
SINGULAR		PLURAL	
ich	hätte	wir	hätten
du	hättest	ihr	hättet
er, sie, es	hätte	sie	hätten
Sie hätten			

ÜBUNG E | **Klamotten kaufen.** You overhear a teenager shopping in a clothing store. He is telling the clerk what he would like. Reconstruct the conversation from the few clues.

EXAMPLE:

> VERKÄUFERIN: was / Sie / gern / haben?   Was hätten Sie gern?
> JUNGE: grau / Pulli   Ich hätte gern einen grauen Pulli.

1. VERKÄUFERIN: welch / Hose / gern haben?

_____

JUNGE: schwarz

_____

2. Verkauferin Gürtel / dazu / gern haben?

_____

Oh ja / schwarz / Gürtel

_____

3. VERKAUFERIN: was / noch / gern haben?

_____

JUNGE: weiß / Hemd

_____

4. VERKAUFERIN: noch / was / gern haben?

_____

JUNGE: noch / dunkelblau / Hose

_____

5. VERKAUFERIN: ?

_____

Junge nein / danke / alles

_____

b. _wäre_ – would be

| **Das wäre nett.** | _That would be nice._ |
| **Wären Sie daran interessiert?** | _Would you be interested in that?_ |

WÄREN		
SINGULAR		PLURAL
ich	wäre	wir wären
du	wärest	ihr wäret
er, sie, es wäre		sie wären
Sie wären		

ÜBUNG F | **Wäre das gut?** Answer Heino's questions with either a positive or negative statement using _wären_. Choose interesting adjectives to reflect your degree of enthusiasm about the idea.

EXAMPLE: Gehen wir morgen in die Stadt? Das wäre (nicht so) schlecht, super, toll, etc.

1. Gehen wir in die Sporthalle? _____

2. Spielen wir Handball? _____

3. Spielen wir Basketball? _____

4. Wir können schwimmen gehen. _____

5. Bleiben wir dort zwei Stunden? _____

c. *würde* – would

Würden is usually used as a helping verb much like *werden*. The infinitive completer goes to the end.

Was würdest du tun?   *What would you do?*
Würden Sie mir bitte helfen?   *Would you please help me?*

Würden is also used with if-clauses.

Was würde er tun, wenn er Millionär wäre?   *What would he do, if he were a millionaire?*
Wenn er ein Auto hätte, würde er uns hinfahren.   *If he had a car, he would drive us.*

WÜRDEN		
SINGULAR		PLURAL
ich würde		wir würden
du würdest		ihr würdet
er, sie, es würde		sie würden
Sie würden		

ÜBUNG G   **Was würdest du machen, wenn...?** You are answering questions for a quiz game on the Internet.

EXAMPLE: Was würdest du machen, wenn du eine Million Dollar hättest?
Ich würde ein neues Auto kaufen.

1. Wenn du in Deutschland wärest? _____

2. Wenn du ein Auto hättest?   _____

3. Wenn du Lehrer wärest?

_____

4. Wenn du in Marbach wärest?

_____

5. Wenn du in München wärest?

_____

d. *möchte* - would like

Möchtest du eine Tasse Tee?   *Would you like a cup of tea?*
Ich möchte mit dir gehen.   *I'd like to go with you.*

MÖCHTEN	
SINGULAR	PLURAL
ich möchte	wir möchten
du möchtest	ihr möchtet
er, sie, es möchte	sie möchten
Sie möchten	

ÜBUNG H | **Eine Umfrage.** Take a survey among your classmates asking them what they would like for their next birthday. Ask at least 5 classmates and record their answers.

EXAMPLE: Was möchtest du, Hans? Ich möchte einen neuen CD-Spieler.

1. _____

2. _____

3. _____

4. _____

5. _____

5.   Verbs with Prepositions

NOTE: Verbs are often used in combination with certain prepositions. The combination never varies. In English one applies *for* a job, is interested *in* something and politicians run *for* office. Similar verb-preposition combinations occur in German. Some of the more common are:

abhängen von + *dat*	*depend upon*
arbeiten an + *dat*	*work an*
sich ärgern über + *acc*	*get angry at*
sich bemühen um + *acc*	*work towards, strive for*
sich beschaftigen mit + *dat*	*be occupied with*
sich bewerben um + *acc*	*apply for*
denken an + *acc*	*think about*
sich freuen auf + *acc*	*look forward to*
sich freuen über + *acc*	*be happy about*
sich gewöhnen an + *acc*	*get used to, get accustomed to*
glauben an + *acc*	*believe in*
sich handeln um + *acc*	*be concerned with, to be about*
sich interessieren für + *acc*	*be interested in*

leiden an + *acc*	*suffer from*
sorgen für + *acc*	*care for*
sich sorgen um + *acc*	*worry about*
teilnehmen an + *dat*	*participate in*
sich verlassen auf + *acc*	*rely upon*
sich verlieben in + *acc*	*fall in love with*
verzichten auf + *acc*	*do without, pass up*
warten auf + *acc*	*wait for*
zweifeln an + *acc*	*have doubts about*

ÜBUNG I **Eine Radtour.** You wrote a message and were not sure of the correct prepositions. Now you can look them up on the list and fill them in.

EXAMPLE: Ich freue mich sehr __auf__ die Pfingstferien nächste Woche.

NOTE: Pfingsten is the seventh Sunday after Easter. Pfingstmontag is a legal holiday in Germany and many schools have a week's Pfingstferien. Because the weather is turning nice after the winter, activities often center around excursions into the country.

Es handelt sich _____ eine kurze Fahrradtour aufs Land. Jetzt beschäftige ich mich _____

meinem Fahrrad. Ich will _____ dieser Tour teilnehmen, aber ich weiß nicht, ob ich mich

_____ mein Rad verlassen kann. Ich möchte nicht _____ die Tour verzichten, also ich

arbeite jetzt _____ meinem Rad. Ich muss es schnell in Ordnung bringen.

ÜBUNG J **Die Radtour.** You have a discussion with your mother about the upcoming bike tour. Use the cues to write your responses.

EXAMPLE: MUTTI: Ich freue nicht auf diese Radtour.
             DU: Warum nicht? Ich habe so lang darauf gewartet.

1. MUTTI: Ich glaube nicht, dass Herr Marzipan der beste Tourleiter ist.

   Du: sich verlassen auf _____

2. MUTTI: Nur, weil er manchmal zu nett zu euch ist. Was machst du jetzt?

   Du: sich beschäftigen _____

   MUTTI: Aber dein Rad ist nagelneu.

3. DU: noch nicht / sich gewöhnen

   Du: aber / doch / sich verlassen

4. MUTTI: Kannst du nicht etwas anderes an dem Wochenende machen?

   DU: nicht verzichten _____

5. MUTTI: Dann sei vorsichtig! Nimm dein Handy und rufe jeden Abend an.

   DU: sich Sorge machen _____

6. MUTTI: Ok, du darfst an der Tour teilnehmen. Denk aber daran, mich oft anzurufen.

   DU: danke / sich verlassen _____

6. Verb-Preposition Combinations with a Subordinate Clause Object

Often the object of the preposition after the verb is not a single noun, but rather a complete clause.

Ich kann mich darauf verlassen, dass du kommen wirst.

I can rely upon the fact that you will come.

When that is the case, the prepositional phrase is completed with a *da*-construction (see page 51), and then the subordinate clause is added. The *da*-construction is often translated in English with the phrase "the fact that."

In the sentence pairs below, the first sentence has an object noun. The second sentence has an object clause and uses the *da*- construction.

Mein Cousin freut sich auf unseren Besuch.   *My cousin is looking forward to our visit.*

Mein Cousin freut sich darauf, dass wir ihn nächste Woche besuchen.

My cousin is looking forward to the fact that we are visiting him next week.

Sie verlässt sich zu sehr auf ihre Mutter.   *She relies too much upon her mother.*

Sie verlässt sich zu sehr darauf, dass ihre Mutter ihr hilft.

She's depending too much upon the fact that her mother will help her.

| ÜBUNG K | **Die nächsten Ferien.** Your classmates are looking forward to the next vacation. Write down what they are looking forward to by using the notes. |

EXAMPLE: Hans / sich freuen auf / dass / er / nicht / zur Schule / gehen / müssen
          Hans freut sich darauf, dass er nicht zur Schule gehen muss.

1. Helena / sich freuen auf / dass / sie / jeden Tag / ins Schwimmbad / gehen / können

   _____

2. Ingo / sich gewöhnen an / dass / er / nicht / vor neun Uhr / aufstehen / müssen

   _____

3. Jasmin / sich verlassen auf / dass / sie / ohne Lernen / in den Ferien / viel Spaß / haben

   _____

4. Patrizia / sich gewöhnen an / wollen / dass / sie / mit keinen Lehrern / reden / müssen

_____

5. Paolo / sich freuen auf / dass / seine Verwandten / zu Besuch / kommen

_____

7. Interrogatives with Verb-Preposition Combinations

If asking a question, the construction is similar. The *wo(r)-* construction replaces the *da(r)-* construction. (See page 52.) If the expected answer to a question is a thing rather than a person, the preposition is completed with *wo-* (or *wor-*) to form the interrogative.

Worauf freust du dich?	*What are you looking forward to?*
Worauf warten Sie?	*What are you waiting for?*
Woran arbeitet dein Professor jetzt?	*What is your professor working on now?*

| ÜBUNG L | **Fragen.** Your grandmother asks you many questions that you must answer.

EXAMPLE: Worauf freust du dich? Ich freue mich auf die Ferien.

1. Womit beschäftigst du dich jetzt?

_____

2. Wofür interessierst du dich eigentlich zur Zeit?

_____

3. Worum sorgst du dich immer?

_____

4. Ich verstehe, aber woran zweifelst du?

_____

5. Worauf wartest du jetzt?

_____

If the expected answer will be a person, rather than a thing, than the correct interrogative pronoun must be used. The distinction between "who" and "whom" is rapidly disappearing in English. It is still made in German. The correct case of the interrogative pronoun must be used when asking a question in German.

INTERROGATIVE PRONOUNS		
NOMINATIVE	*who*	**wer**
DATIVE	*whom*	**wen**
ACCUSATIVE	*whom*	**wem**

Auf wen wartest du?   *For whom are you waiting?*

In wen hat deine Schwester sich verliebt?   *With whom did your sister fall in love?*

ÜBUNG M   **Omas Fragen.** You are getting ready to go out in the evening. Your grandmother is now asking you lots of questions. What possible answers could you give her? Don't be afraid to use two-clause sentences in some of your answers.

EXAMPLE: Auf wen wartest du?
            Ich warte auf Jon. Wir gehen ins Kino.

1. OMA: Womit beschäftigst du dich jetzt?

   DU: _____

2. OMA: Auf wen verlässt du dich immer?

   DU: _____

3. OMA: Auf wen freust du dich?

   DU: _____

4. OMA: Worauf freust du dich?

   DU: _____

5. OMA: Kannst du dich woran gewöhnen?

   DU: _____

6. OMA: Wogegen (oder wofür) kämpft die Organization „Greenpeace"?

   DU: _____

ÜBUNG N   **Ein Interview.** For an article in the school newspaper you are doing an interview with a typical student. To prepare for the interview write out the questions and some possible answers.

EXAMPLE: sich freuen auf   Worauf freust du dich?
            Ich freue mich auf die Ferien.

1. sich interessieren für?

   _____

   Ich _____

2. Warum / das / sich interessieren für?

   _____

   Weil _____

3. nicht / verzichten auf / wollen?

   _____

   Ich _____

4. warum / das / nicht / verzichten auf / wollen

   _____

   Weil_____

5. sich / sorgen um?

   _____

   Ich _____

6. warum / sich sorgen um?

   _____

   Weil _____

7. sich beschäftigen mit?

   _____

   Ich _____

ÜBUNG O **Die letzte Übung!** You've completed two levels of grammar exercises. Now it's time to write a good autobiography. Be creative. Use sentences with reflexives and subordinate clauses. Vary your word order. Use modals, *da-* and *wo-*constructions, and conditionals (*hätte, wäre, möchte* and *würde*). Make your autobiography as interesting as you are.

_____

_____

_____

_____

_____

_____

_____

_____

_____

_____

Appendix – Grammar Reference Tables

1. Weak Verbs – Conjugation

hören- *to hear*

		ACTIVE VOICE
PRESENT TENSE	ich	**hör**e
	du	**hör**st
	er, sie, es	**hör**t
	wir	**hör**en
	ihr	**hör**t
	sie, Sie	**hör**en
PAST TENSE	ich	**hör**te
	du	**hör**test
	er, sie, es	**hör**te
	wir	**hör**ten
	ihr	**hör**tet
	sie, Sie	**hör**ten
FUTURE TENSE	ich	**werde** hören
	du	**wirst** hören
	er, sie, es	**wird** hören
	wir	**werden** hören
	ihr	**werdet** hören
	sie, Sie	**werden** hören
PRESENT PERFECT TENSE	ich	**habe** gehört
	du	**hast** gehört
	er, sie, es	**hat** gehört
	wir	**haben** gehört
	ihr	**hab**t gehört
	sie, Sie	**haben** gehört

		ACTIVE VOICE
PAST PERFECT TENSE	ich	**hatte** gehört
	du	**hattest** gehört
	er, sie, es	**hatte** gehört
	wir	**hatten** gehört
	ihr	**hattet** gehört
	sie, Sie	**hatten** gehört
FUTURE PERFECT TENSE	ich	**werde** gehört **haben**
	du	**wirst** gehört **haben**
	er, sie, es	**wird** gehört **haben**
	wir	**werden** gehört **haben**
	ihr	**werdet** gehört **haben**
	sie, Sie	**werden** gehört **haben**
IMPERATIVE	du	Hör(e)!
	wir	Hören wir!
	ihr	Hört!
	Sie	Hören Sie!

2.   Strong Verbs (Auxiliary Verb = *haben*)

tragen, trägt, trug, hat getragen - to wear or carry

		ACTIVE VOICE
PRESENT TENSE	ich	trag**e**
	du	tr**ä**g**st**
	er, sie, es	tr**ä**g**t**
	wir	trag**en**
	ihr	trag**t**
	sie, Sie	trag**en**
PAST TENSE	ich	trug
	du	trug**st**
	er, sie, es	trug
	wir	trug**en**
	ihr	trug**t**
	sie, Sie	trug**en**

		ACTIVE VOICE
FUTURE TENSE	ich	**werde** tragen
	du	**wirst** tragen
	er, sie, es	**wird** tragen
	wir	**werden** tragen
	ihr	**werdet** tragen
	sie, Sie	**werden** tragen
PRESENT PERFECT TENSE	ich	**habe** getragen
	du	**hast** getragen
	er, sie, es	**hat** getragen
	wir	**haben** getragen
	ihr	**habt** getragen
	sie, Sie	**haben** getragen
PAST PERFECT TENSE	ich	**hatte** getragen
	du	**hattest** getragen
	er, sie, es	**hatte** getragen
	wir	**hatten** getragen
	ihr	**hattet** getragen
	sie, Sie	**hatten** getragen
FUTURE PERFECT TENSE	ich	**werde** getragen **haben**
	du	**wirst** getragen **haben**
	er, sie, es	**wird** getragen **haben**
	wir	**werden** getragen **haben**
	ihr	**werdet** getragen **haben**
	sie, Sie	**werden** getragen **haben**
IMPERATIVE	du	Trag(e)!
	wir	Tragen wir!
	ihr	Tragt!
	Sie	Tragen Sie!

3.   Strong Verbs (Auxiliary Verb = *sein*)

gehen, geht, ging, ist gegangen – to go

		ACTIVE VOICE
PRESENT TENSE	ich	geh**e**
	du	geh**st**
	er, sie, es	geh**t**
	wir	geh**en**
	ihr	geh**t**
	sie, Sie	geh**en**
PAST TENSE	ich	ging
	du	ging**st**
	er, sie, es	ging
	wir	ging**en**
	ihr	ging**t**
	sie, Sie	ging**en**
FUTURE TENSE	ich	**werde** gehen
	du	**wirst** gehen
	er, sie, es	**wird** gehen
	wir	**werden** gehen
	ihr	**werdet** gehen
	sie, Sie	**werden** gehen
PRESENT PERFECT TENSE	ich	**bin** gegangen
	du	**bist** gegangen
	er, sie, es	**ist** gegangen
	wir	**sind** gegangen
	ihr	**seid** gegangen
	sie, Sie	**sind** gegangen
PAST PERFECT TENSE	ich	**war** gegangen
	du	**warst** gegangen
	er, sie, es	**war** gegangen
	wir	**waren** gegangen
	ihr	**wart** gegangen
	sie, Sie	**waren** gegangen

		ACTIVE VOICE	
FUTURE PERFECT TENSE	ich	**werde** gegangen **sein**	
	du	**wirst** gegangen **sein**	
	er, sie, es	**wird** gegangen **sein**	
	wir	**werden** gegangen **sein**	
	ihr	**werdet** gegangen **sein**	
	sie, Sie	**werden** gegangen **sein**	
IMPERATIVE	du	Geh(e)!	
	wir	Gehen wir!	
	ihr	Geht!	
	Sie	Gehen Sie!	

4.   Strong Verbs – List of Principal Parts

		PRINCIPAL PARTS OF STRONG VERBS		
INFINITIVE	PRESENT TENSE THIRD PERSON SINGULAR	PAST TENSE FIRST AND THIRD PERSONS SINGULAR	PAST PARTICIPLE WITH AUXILIARY VERB	ENGLISH MEANING
backen	bäckt	backte (buk)	hat gebacken	bake
befehlen	befiehlt	befahl	hat befohlen	command
beginnen	beginnt	begann	hat begonnen	begin
beißen	beißt	biss	hat gebissen	bite
bergen	birgt	barg	hat geborgen	hide, protect
betrügen	betrügt	betrog	hat betrogen	betray, deceive
biegen	biegt	bog	hat/ist gebogen	bend, turn
bieten	bietet	bot	hat geboten	offer
binden	bindet	band	hat gebunden	tie, bind
bitten	bittet	bat	hat gebeten	request, plea
blasen	bläst	blies	hat geblasen	blow
bleiben	bleibt	blieb	ist geblieben	stay, remain
braten	brät	briet	hat gebraten	roast, fry
brechen	bricht	brach	hat gebrochen	break
brennen	brennt	brannte	hat gebrannt	burn
bringen	bringt	brachte	hat gebracht	bring

INFINITIVE	PRESENT TENSE THIRD PERSON SINGULAR	PAST TENSE FIRST AND THIRD PERSONS SINGULAR	PAST PARTICIPLE WITH AUXILIARY VERB	ENGLISH MEANING
denken	denkt	dachte	hat gedacht	think
dringen	dringt	drang	hat/ist gedrungen	press forward
dürfen	darf	durfte	hat gedurft	may, be allowed to
empfehlen	empfiehlt	empfahl	hat empfohlen	recommend
erschrecken	erschrickt	erschrak	ist erschrocken	be startled
essen	isst	aß	hat gegessen	eat
fahren	fährt	fuhr	hat/ist gefahren	ride, drive
fallen	fällt	fiel	ist gefallen	fall
fangen	fängt	fing	hat gefangen	catch
findet	findet	fand	hat gefunden	find
fliegen	fliegt	flog	hat/ist geflogen	fly
fliehen	flieht	floh	ist geflohen	flee
fließen	fließt	floss	ist geflossen	flow
fressen	frisst	fraß	hat gefressen	eat (animal), devour
frieren	friert	fror	hat/ist gefroren	freeze
gebären	gebärt	gebar	hat geboren	give birth to
geben	gibt	gab	hat gegeben	give
gedeihen	gedeiht	gedieh	ist gediehen	grow, thrive
gehen	geht	ging	ist gegangen	go, walk
gelingen	gelingt	gelang	ist gelungen	succeed
gelten	gilt	galt	hat gegolten	be valid
genießen	genießt	genoss	hat genossen	enjoy
geschehen	geschieht	geschah	ist geschehen	happen
gewinnen	gewinnt	gewann	hat gewonnen	win
gießen	gießt	goss	hat gegossen	pour
gleichen	gleicht	glich	hat geglichen	resemble
gleiten	gleitet	glitt	ist geglitten	glide, slide
graben	gräbt	grub	hat gegraben	dig
greifen	greift	griff	hat gegriffen	grasp, grab
haben	hat	hatte	hat gehabt	have
halten	hält	hielt	hat gehalten	hold, stop
hängen	hängt	hing	hat gehangen	hang

INFINITIVE	PRESENT TENSE THIRD PERSON SINGULAR	PAST TENSE FIRST AND THIRD PERSONS SINGULAR	PAST PARTICIPLE WITH AUXILIARY VERB	ENGLISH MEANING
hauen	haut	haute	hat gehauen	cut
heben	hebt	hob	hat gehoben	life, raise up
heißen	heißt	hieß	hat geheißen	be called
helfen	hilft	half	hat geholfen	help
kennen	kennt	kannte	hat gekonnt	know, be acquainted with
klingen	klingt	klang	hat geklungen	sound
kneifen	kneift	kniff	hat gekniffen	pinch
kommen	kommt	kam	ist gekommen	come
können	kann	konnte	hat gekonnt	can, be able to
kriechen	kriecht	kroch	ist gekrochen	crawl
laden	lädt	lud	hat geladen	load
lassen	lässt	ließ	hat gelassen	let, leave, allow
laufen	läuft	lief	ist gelaufen	run, walk
leiden	leidet	litt	hat gelitten	suffer
lesen	liest	las	hat gelesen	read
liegen	liegt	lag	hat gelegen	lie
mahlen	mahlt	mahlte	hat gemahlen	grind
meiden	meidet	mied	hat gemieden	avoid
messen	misst	maß	hat gemessen	measure
misslingen	misslingt	misslang	ist misslungen	fail
mögen	mag	mochte	hat gemocht	like, like to
müssen	muss	musste	hat gemusst	must, have to
nehmen	nimmt	nahm	hat genommen	take
nennen	nennt	nannte	hat genannt	name
pfeifen	pfeift	pfiff	hat gepfiffen	whistle
preisen	preist	pries	hat gepriesen	praise
raten	rät	riet	hat geraten	advise, guess
reiben	reibt	rieb	hat gerieben	rub
reißen	reißt	riss	hat/ist gerissen	rip, tear
reiten	reitet	ritt	hat/ist geritten	ride (an animal)
rennen	rennt	rannte	ist gerannt	run

INFINITIVE	PRESENT TENSE THIRD PERSON SINGULAR	PAST TENSE FIRST AND THIRD PERSONS SINGULAR	PAST PARTICIPLE WITH AUXILIARY VERB	ENGLISH MEANING
riechen	riecht	roch	hat gerochen	smell
ringen	ringt	rang	hat gerungen	wrestle
rufen	ruft	rief	hat gerufen	call
salzen	salzt	salzte	hat gesalzen	salt
saufen	säuft	soff	hat gesoffen	drink (animal)
schaffen	schafft	schuf	hat geschaffen	create, accomplish
scheiden	scheidet	schied	hat/ist geschieden	separate
scheinen	scheint	schien	hat geschienen	shine, seem
schieben	schieb	schob	hat geschoben	shove, push
schießen	schießt	schoss	hat geschossen	shoot
schlafen	schläft	schlief	hat geschlafen	sleep
schlagen	schlägt	schlug	hat geschlagen	hit, beat
schleichen	schleicht	schlich	ist geschlichen	creep
schließen	schließt	schloss	hat geschlossen	close, end
schmeißen	schmeißt	schmiss	hat geschmissen	throw out, chuck
schmelzen	schmilzt	schmolz	hat geschmolzen	melt
schneiden	schneidet	schnitt	hat geschnitten	cut
schreiben	schreibt	schrieb	hat geschrieben	write
schreien	schreit	schrie	hat geschrien	scream, shout
schreiten	schreitet	schritt	ist geschritten	stride
schweigen	schweigt	schwieg	hat geschwiegen	be silent
schwimmen	schwimmt	schwamm	hat/ist geschwommen	swim
schwingen	schwingt	schwang	ist geschwungen	swing
sehen	sieht	sah	hat gesehen	see
sein	ist	war	ist gewesen	be
senden	sendet	sandte	hat gesandt	send, deploy
singen	singt	sang	hat gesungen	sing
sinken	sinkt	sank	hat gesunken	sink
sitzen	sitzt	saß	hat gesessen	sit
sollen	soll	sollte	hat gesollt	should, supposed to
spinnen	spinnt	spann	hat gesponnen	be silly, tell tall tales
sprechen	spricht	sprach	hat gesprochen	speak

INFINITIVE	PRESENT TENSE THIRD PERSON SINGULAR	PAST TENSE FIRST AND THIRD PERSONS SINGULAR	PAST PARTICIPLE WITH AUXILIARY VERB	ENGLISH MEANING
springen	springt	sprang	ist gesprungen	jump, spring
stechen	sticht	stach	hat gestochen	stick, prick
stehen	steht	stand	hat gestanden	stand
stehlen	stiehlt	stahl	hat gestohlen	steal
steigen	steigt	stieg	ist gestiegen	climb
sterben	stirbt	starb	ist gestorben	die
stinken	stinkt	stank	hat gestunken	smell bad
stoßen	stößt	stieß	hat/ist gestoßen	bump, push
streichen	streicht	strich	hat gestrichen	stroke, pet, paint
streiten	streitet	stritt	hat gestritten	quarrel, argue
tragen	trägt	trug	hat getragen	carry, wear
treffen	trifft	traf	hat getroffen	meet
treiben	treibt	trieb	hat getrieben	drive
trinken	trinkt	trank	hat getrunken	drink
tun	tut	tat	hat getan	do
verbieten	verbietet	verbot	hat verboten	forbid
verderben	verdirbt	verdarb	hat/ist verdorben	spoil
vergessen	vergisst	vergaß	hat vergessen	forget
verlieren	verliert	verlor	hat verloren	lose
verzeihen	verzeiht	verzieh	hat verziehen	forgive
wachsen	wächst	wuchs	ist gewachsen	grow
waschen	wäscht	wusch	hat gewaschen	wash
weichen	weicht	wich	ist gewichen	yield
weisen	weist	wies	hat gewiesen	point
werben	wirbt	warb	hat geworben	advertise
werden	wird	wurde	ist geworden	become, will
werfen	wirft	warf	hat geworfen	throw
wiegen	wiegt	wog	hat gewogen	weigh
wissen	weiß	wusste	hat gewusst	know (a fact)
wollen	will	wollte	hat gewollt	want, want to
ziehen	zieht	zog	hat gezogen	pull
zwingen	zwingt	zwang	hat gezwungen	force

5.   Dative Verbs

The following verbs take dative direct objects.

abraten, rät ab, riet ab, hat abgeraten (von + dat)	*advise against*
ähneln	*resemble*
antworten	*answer*
ausweichen, weicht aus, wich aus, ist ausgewichen	*avoid, get out of the way*
begegnen	*meet*
beistehen, steht bei, stand bei, hat beigestanden	*support, stand behind*
beitreten, tritt bei, trat bei, ist beigetreten	*join*
bekommen, bekommt, bekam, hat bekommen	*agree with (food)*
danken	*thank*
dienen	*serve*
drohen	*threaten*
einfallen, fällt ein, fiel ein, ist eingefallen	*occur*
entgegenkommen, kommt entgegen, kam entgegen, ist entgegengekommen	*come towards*
folgen (ist)	*follow*
gehorchen	*obey*
gehören	*belong to*
gelten, gilt, galt, hat gegolten	*be meant for, be valid*
gleichen, gleicht, glich, hat geglichen	*be the same as, resemble*
gratulieren	*congratulate*
helfen, hilft, half, hat geholfen	*help*
imponieren	*impress*
nachahmen	*mock, ape, copy*
passen	*fit*
schaden	*harm*
schmeicheln	*flatter*
trauen	*trust*
vertrauen	*have trust or confidence in*
wehtun, tut weh, tat weh, hat wehgetan	*hurt*
widersprechen, widerspricht, widersprach, hat widersprochen	*contradict*
zuhören	*listen to*

6.   Definite and Indefinite Articles

DEFINITE ARTICLES				
	SINGULAR			PLURAL
	MASCULINE	FEMININE	NEUTER	
NOMINATIVE	der	die	das	die
DATIVE	dem	der	dem	den
ACCUSATIVE	den	die	das	die

INDEFINITE ARTICLES				
	SINGULAR			PLURAL
	MASCULINE	FEMININE	NEUTER	
NOMINATIVE	ein	eine	ein	keine
DATIVE	einem	einer	einem	keinen
ACCUSATIVE	einen	eine	ein	keine

7.   Adjective Endings

COMPARISON OF WEAK, STRONG, AND MIXED ADJECTIVE ENDINGS				
	SINGULAR			PLURAL
	MASCULINE	FEMININE	NEUTER	
Nom. weak	der alt-e	die alt-e	das alt-e	die alt-en
mixed	ein alt-er	eine alt-e	ein alt-es	keine alt-en
strong	alt-er	alt-e	alt-es	alt-e
Dat. weak	dem alt-en	der alt-en	dem alt-en	den alt-en
mixed	einem alt-en	einer alt-en	einem alt-en	keinen alt-en
strong	alt-em	alt-er	alt-em	alt-en
Acc. weak	den alt-en	die alt-e	das alt-e	die alt-en
mixed	einen alt-en	eine alt-e	ein alt-es	keine alt-en
strong	alt-en	alt-e	alt-es	alt-e
Gen. weak	des alt-en	der alt-en	des alt-en	der alt-en
mixed	eines alt-en	einer alt-e	eines alt-en	keiner alt-en
strong	alt-en	alt-er	alt-en	alt-er

German-English Vocabulary

Abbreviations used in this glossary

acc. – accusative

dat. – dative

fam. – familiar

fem. – feminine

prep. dat./prep. acc. – preposition which takes the dative/accusative case

pol. – polite formal

sep. prefix – separable prefix

pl. – plural

s.o. – some one

s.t. – something

v.t. – transitive verb (verb that can take a direct object and usually uses **haben** to form the perfect tenses)

v.i. – intransitive verb (verb that cannot take a direct object and usually uses **sein** to form the perfect tenses)

A

ab und zu every now and then

abbiegen, biegt ab, bog ab, hat abgebogen *sep. prefix* turn off (at a street)

der Abend, *pl.* **-e** evening

das Abendessen, *pl.* **-** dinner, evening meal

abends evenings, in the evening

abenteuerlich adventuresome

aber but, however

abfahren, fährt ab, fuhr ab, ist abgefahren, *v.i., sep. prefix* depart, drive away

abhängen von + dat, hängt ab, hing ab, hat abgehangen *sep. prefix* depend upon

abholen *sep. prefix* pick up, fetch

abhören *sep. prefix* listen to, quiz verbally

abputzen *sep. prefix* clean

die Abreise, -n departure

abspülen *sep. prefix* to wash the dishes

acht eight

ähneln resemble, be similar to

ähnlich *sep. prefix* similar

die Ahnung, *pl.* **-en** premonition; idea

akkurat accurate

die Alexanderkirche, *pl.* **-en** Alexander Church

alle all

alles everything; all

das Alphabet, *pl.* **-e** alphabet

als when

alt old

altmodisch old fashioned

die Altstadt, *pl.* **-¨e** old town; old quarter of the city

amerikanisch American

die Ampel, *pl.* **-n** traffic light

an on

das Andenken, *pl.* **-** souvenir

anders different

anfangen, fängt an, fing an, hat angefangen *sep. prefix* to begin

der Angeber, *pl.* **-** braggart

angeln to fish

die Angst, *pl.* **-¨e** worry

anhaben, hat an, hatte an, hat angehabt to have on

ankommen, kommt an, kam an, ist angekommen, *v.i., sep. prefix* to arrive

anprobieren *sep. prefix* to try on

anrufen, ruft an, rief an, hat angerufen, *v.t., sep. prefix* to call up

anschauen, *v.t., sep. prefix* to look at

ansehen, sieht an, sah an, hat angesehen *sep. prefix* to look at

die Ansichtskarte, *pl.* **-en** postcard

Antwort, *pl.* **-en** answer

antworten to answer

die Anweisungen directions

anziehen, zieht an, zog an, hat angezogen *sep. prefix* to put on

der Anzug, *pl.* **-ˮe** suit

der Apfel, *pl.* **-ˮ** apple

der Apfelsaft, *pl.* **-ˮe** apple juice

die Apfelschorle, *pl.* **-en** apple juice with seltzer

die Apotheke, *pl.* **-en** pharmacist

die Arbeit, *pl.* **-en** work

arbeiten to work

arbeiten an + *acc.* to work on

der Ärger annoyance; anger

ärgerlich annoying

ärgern to make angry; to annoy

arm poor

der Arme, *pl.* **-n** poor man

die Ärztin, *pl.* **-nen** female doctor

der Atem breath

auch also

auf up; on top of

Auf Wiedersehen goodbye

aufbleiben, bleibt auf, blieb auf, ist aufgeblieben *sep. prefix* stay up; stay open

die Aufgabe, *pl.* **-n** homework

das Aufgabenheft, *pl.* **-e** notebook for homework

die Aufgabenliste, *pl.* **-n** list of assignments

aufgehen, geht auf, ging auf, ist aufgegangen *sep. prefix* to rise

aufhören *sep. prefix* to stop doing (something)

auflegen *sep. prefix* to hang up the phone; lay *s.t.* on top of *s.t.*

aufmachen *sep. prefix* to open

aufräumen, *v.t., sep. prefix* to clean up

aufregend exciting

aufschlagen, schlägt auf, schlug auf, hat aufgeschlagen *sep. prefix* to set up; to open

aufschreiben, schreibt auf, schrieb auf, hat aufgeschrieben *sep. prefix* to write down

aufstehen, steht auf, stand auf, hat aufgestanden *sep. prefix* to stand up

das Auge, *pl.* **-n** eye

der August August

aus *prep. dat.* from; out of

der Ausflug, *pl.* **-ˮe** excursion, trip

das Ausflugsvideo, *pl.* **-s** trip video

ausgeben, gibt aus, gab aus, hat ausgegeben *sep. prefix* to hand out

ausgehen, geht aus, ging aus, ist ausgegangen *sep. prefix* to go out

ausgezeichnet excellent

die Auskunft, *pl.* **-ˮe** information

auspacken, *v.t., sep. prefix* to unpack

ausrollen, *v.t., sep. prefix* to unroll

aussehen, sieht aus, sah aus, hat ausgesehen *sep. prefix* to look (appearance)

außer *prep. dat.* besides; except for

auswischen *sep. prefix* to wipe out

ausziehen, zieht aus, zog aus, hat ausgezogen *sep. prefix* to take off

das Auto, *pl.* **-s** car

der Autoverkehr traffic

die Autoversicherung, *pl.* **-en** car insurance

B

der Bäcker, *pl.* **-** baker

die Bäckerei, *pl.* **-n** bakery

die Badehose, *pl.* **-n** swimming trunks

baden to swim, to bathe; to take a bath

die Bahn, *pl.* **-en** train

der Bahnhof, *pl.* **-ˮe** train station

die Bahnhofsbrücke, *pl.* **-n** railroad bridge

bald soon

die Bank, *pl.* **-en** bank; (finance)

die Bank, die Bänke bench

die Bankkarte, *pl.* **-n** bank card

der Bär, *pl.* **-en** bear

der Basketball, *pl.* **-ˮe** basketball

das Basketballspiel, *pl.* **-e** basketball game

der Bauch; *pl.* **-e** stomach; belly

der Bauernhof, *pl.* **-ˮe** farm

der Baum, *pl.* **-ˮe** tree

befehlen, befiehlt, befahl, hat befohlen to order; to command

beginnen, beginnt, begann, hat begonnen to begin

behalten, behält, behielt, hat behalten to keep; to remember

bei *prep. dat.* at the house of; near

beim (=bei + dem) at the home of; at the

das Bein, *pl.* **-e** leg

beißen, beißt, biss, hat gebissen to bite

bekannt known

bellen to bark

bemühen um to work towards; to strive for
das Benehmen behavior
der Berg, *pl.* **-e** mountain
der Bericht, *pl.* **-e** report
berichten to report
berühmt known
beschäftigen mit + *dat.* to be occupied with
die Beschreibung, *pl.* **-en** description
besichtigen to visit an attraction; tour *s.t.*
besitzen, besitzt, besaß, hat besessen to own; to possess
besorgen to own; to possess
die Besorgung, *pl.* **-en** errand
besprechen, bespricht, besprach, hat besprochen to discuss
besser better
der Beste, *pl.* **-n** best
der Besuch, *pl.* **-e** visit
besuchen, *v.t.* to visit
Bett, *pl.* **-en** bed
bevor before
bewerben um + *acc.* to apply for
bezaubernd enchanted
die Bibliothek, *pl.* **-en** library
biegen biegt, bog, hat gebogen to bend
die Biene, *pl.* **-en** bee
das Bier, *pl.* **-e** beer
das Bild, *pl.* **-er** picture
das Bilderbuch, *pl.* **-ʺer** picture book
die Birne, *pl.* **-n** pear
bis *prep. acc.* until; up to
bisschen a little
bitte please
das Blasquartett, *pl.* **-e** wind quartet
blau blue
bleiben, bleibt, blieb, ist geblieben to stay; to remain
die Blume, *pl.* **-n** flower

die Bluse, *pl.* **-n** blouse
der Boden, *pl.* **-ʺ** floor
das Boot, *pl.* **-e** boat
böse angry
brauchen to need
braun brown
brav good; well-behaved
brechen, bricht, brach, hat gebrochen to break
breit wide
der Brief, *pl.* **-e** letter
die Brille, *pl.* **-n** eyeglasses
bringen, bringt, brach, hat gebracht to bring
der Broccoli broccoli
die Broschüre, *pl.* **-n** brochure
das Brot, *pl.* **-e** bread
das Brötchen, *pl.* **-** roll (bread)
die Brücke, *pl.* **-n** bridge
der Bruder, *pl.* **-ʺ** brother
die Brust, *pl.* **-ʺe** chest; breast
das Buch, *pl.* **-ʺer** book
der Buchbericht, *pl.* **-e** book report
die Buchhandlung, *pl.* **-en** book store
der Büffel, *pl.* buffalo
bunt colorful
der Bürgermeister, *pl.* **-** mayor
der Burgplatz, *pl.* **-ʺe** town square in front of a castle
bürsten to brush
der Bus, *pl.* **-se** bus

C

das Café, *pl.* **-s** café
die Campingabteilung, *pl.* **-en** camping supplies department
der Campingplatz, *pl.* **-ʺe** campground
die Campingreise, *pl.* **-n** camping trip
die CD, *pl.* **-s** CD
CD-Laden, *pl.* **-ʺ** CD shop

der CD-Spieler, *pl.* CD player
der Charakter, *pl.* **-e** character
die Checkliste, *pl.* **-n** checklist
der Chihuahua chihuahua; Mexican dog
der Clown, *pl.* **-s** clown
die Cola, *pl.* **-s (also acceptable das Cola,** *pl.* **-s)** cola
der Computer computer
die Couch, *pl.* **-s/-en** couch
der Cousin, *pl.* **-s** male cousin
die Cousine, *pl.* **-n** female cousin

D

der Dachshund, *pl.* **-e** dachsund
damit with (it or them)
danach after it; there
der Dank thanks
danken to thank
dann then
daraus out of it; out of them; from it; from them
dass that
dauern to last
dauernd constant
die Decke, *pl.* **-n** cover; tablecloth
decken to cover; to lay; to set
dein your *fam.*
denken, denkt, dachte, hat gedacht to think
denken an + *acc.* to think about
das Denkmal, *pl.* **-ʺer** monument
denn because
deutsch German
das Deutsch German language
das Deutschbuch, *pl.* **-ʺer** German book

Deutsche Dogge, *pl.* **-n**
great dane
das Deutschland Germany
der Dezember December
dich you *fam. acc.*
dick thick; fat
der Dieb, -e thief
der Dienstag, -e Tuesday
dies this
dieser this
dir to you *fam. dat.*
direkt direct
die Disco, *pl.* **-s** discotheque
doch but; yet
der Doktor, *pl.* **-en** doctor
der Dom, *pl.* **-e** cathedral
der Donnerstag, *pl.* **-e**
Thursday
das Dorf, *pl.* **-ˮer** village
das Dorfmuseum, die
Dorfmuseen village
museum
dort there
dort drüben over there
der Drache, *pl.* **-n** dragon
dran on it; on them
der Dreh, *pl.* **-s** spin **(im**
Dreh) spinning
drei three
die Drogerie, *pl.* **-n** drug
store
drüben over there
du you *fam.*
dumm stupid
dunkelblau dark blue
dünn thin
durch *prep. acc.* through
das Durcheinander, *pl.* **-s**
muddle
dürfen, darf, durfte, hat
gedurft to be allowed to;
may
die Dusche, *pl.* **-n** shower
duschen to take a shower

E
echt real
die Ecke, *pl.* **-n** corner
das ist egal I don't care

eher earlier; sooner
eigentlich actually
ein a(n); one
einbiegen, biegt ein, bog
ein, ist eingebogen *sep.*
prefix turn (into a street)
eines Tages one day
einfallen, fällt ein, fiel ein,
ist eingefallen *sep. prefix*
to occur to
einige unique; only
einkaufen *sep. prefix* to shop
das Einkaufen shopping
die Einkaufsliste, *pl.* **-n**
shopping list
einladen, lädt ein, lud ein,
hat eingeladen *sep. prefix*
to invite
die Einladung, *pl.* **-en**
invitation
einlegen *sep. prefix* to put in;
to lay
die Eintrittskarte, *pl.* **-n**
ticket
das Eis ice cream
das Eiscafé, *pl.* **-s** ice cream
parlor
eiskalt ice cold
der Elefant, *pl.* **-en** elephant
elf eleven
die Eltern, *pl.* parents
die E-Mail (often written
Email; das Email in
Southern Germany), *pl.* **-s**
e-mail
endlich finally
englisch English
das Englisch English
language
entlang along
er he
die Erbse, *pl.* **-n** pea
der Erfolg, *pl.* **-e** success
erfolgreich successful
erhofft hoped for
erkälten to catch a cold
erlauben to allow; to permit
das Erlebnis, *pl.* **-se**
experience

erledigen, *v.t.* to finish
die Erinnerung, *pl.* **-en**
memory
erscheinen, erscheint,
erschien, ist erschienen
to appear suddenly
ersetzen to replace
erst first; only
erzählen to tell
es it
der Esel, - donkey
essen, isst, aß, hat gegessen,
v.t. to eat
das Essen, - food
etwas something; anything
euch you
euer your *fam. pl.*

F
fahren, fährt, fuhr, ist
gefahren *v.i.* to travel
die Fahrkarte, *pl.* **-n** ticket
der Fahrplan, *pl.* **-ˮe**
timetable
das Fahrrad, *pl.* **-ˮer** bicycle
die Fahrradtour, *pl.* **-en**
bicycle tour
die Fahrschule, *pl.* **-n**
driving school
fair fair
fallen, fällt, fiel, ist gefallen
to fall
die Familie, *pl.* **-n** family
fangen, fängt, fing hat
gefangen to catch
das Fantasiebuch, *pl.* **-ˮer**
fantasy book
fantastisch fantastic
der Farbfernseher, *pl.* **-** color
TV
farbig colorful
fast almost
faul lazy
der Februar, *pl.* **-** February
fehlen to be missing
das Feld, *pl.* **-er** meadow
die Ferien, *pl.* vacation
das Ferienbild, *pl.* **-er**
vacation photos

der Ferientag, *pl.* **-e** vacation day

fernsehen, sieht fern, sah fern, hat ferngesehen to watch TV

der Fernseher, *pl.* **-** TV

der Fernwanderer, *pl.* **-** long distance hiker

fertig ready

der Film, *pl.* **-e** film

finden, findet, fand, hat gefunden to find

der Fisch, *pl.* **-e** fish

das Fitnesstraining, *pl.* **-s** fitness training

die Flasche, *pl.* **-en** bottle

fleißig hard-working

fliegen, fliegt, flog, ist geflogen to fly

der Flohmarkt, *pl.* **-̈e** flea market

der Flughafen, *pl.* **-̈** airport

der Fluss, *pl.* **-̈e** river

folgen (ist gefolgt) to follow

das Folklore-Konzert, *pl.* **-e** folklore concert

die Forelle, *pl.* **-n** trout

die Fortsetzung, *pl.* **-en** continuation

das Foto, *pl.* **-s** photo

das Fotoalbum, die Fotoalben photo album

fotografieren to take a picture of

die Frage, *pl.* **-n** question

die Frau, *pl.* **-n** woman

das Freiluftkonzert, *pl.* **-e** outdoor concert

der Freitag, *pl.* **-e** Friday

fremd strange; foreign

die Freude, *pl.* **-n** joy

freuen to please

der Freund, *pl.* **-e** male friend

die Freundin, *pl.* **-nen** female friend

freundlich friendly

der Friedhof, *pl.* **-̈e** cemetery

frisch fresh

der Friseursalon, *pl.* **-s** beauty parlor

früh early

der Frühling, *pl.* **-e** spring

das Frühstück, *pl.* **-e** breakfast

frühstücken to eat breakfast

das Fundbüro, *pl.* **-s** lost and found

der Fünfklässler, *pl.* **-** fifth grader

für *prep. acc.* for

furchtbar terrible

der Fuß, die Füsse foot; feet

der Fußball, *pl.* **-̈e** soccer

der Fußballplatz, *pl.* **-̈e** soccer field

das Fußballspiel, *pl.* **-e** soccer game

füttern to feed (an animal)

G

die Gabel, *pl.* **-n** spoon

gackern to cackle

ganz totally; completely

der Garten, *pl.* **-̈** garden

der Gasthof, *pl.* **-̈e** guest house; inn

das Gebäude, *pl.* **-** building

geben, gibt, gab, hat gegeben to give

gebrauchen to use

gebrochen broken

das Geburtshaus, *pl.* **-̈er** birth house

der Geburtstag, *pl.* **-e** birthday

das Gedicht, *pl.* **-e** poem

die Geduld patience

gefallen, gefällt, gefiel, hat gefallen to please; to be pleasing

die Gefühlskarte, *pl.* **-en** *prep. acc.* card illustrating an emotion

gegen against

die Gegend, *pl.* **-en** area

gegenüber across from; opposite

gegeneinander against each other

gehen, geht, ging, ist gegangen, *v.i.* to go

gehorchen to obey

gehören to listen

gehorsam obedient

gelb yellow

das Geld, -er money

gelingen, gelingt, gelang, ist gelungen to succeed

das Gemüse, *pl.* **-** vegetables

die Gemüsesuppe, *pl.* **-n** vegetable soup

gemütlich cozy

genau exactly

genießen, genießt, genoß, hat genossen to enjoy

genug enough

der Gepard, *pl.* **-e** cheetah

geradeaus straight ahead

gern(e) with pleasure

das Geschäft, *pl.* **-e** store

geschehen, geschieht, geschah, ist geschehen to happen

das Geschenk, *pl.* **-e** gift

Geschichte, *pl.* **-n** story; history

das Gesicht, *pl.* **-er** face

das Gespräch, *pl.* **-e** conversation

gestern yesterday

gestreift striped

gesund healthy

die Gesundheit health

das Getränk, *pl.* **-e** drink

gewinnen, gewinnt, gewann, hat gewonnen to win

die Giraffe, *pl.* **-n** giraffe

das Glas, *pl.* **-̈er** glass

der Glas-Recycling-Tag, *pl.* **-e** glass recycling day

**glauben an + ** *acc.* to believe in

gleich same, similar

gleichzeitig at the same time

das Glockenspiel, *pl.* **-e** glockenspiel

glücklich lucky

der Goldfisch, *pl.* **-e** goldfish

der Gorilla, *pl.* **-s** gorilla

der Gott, *pl.* **-¨er** God; god

die Grammatik, *pl.* **-en** grammar

gratulieren to congratulate

die Grippe flu

groß large; big

die Großeltern, *pl.* grandparents

die Großmutter, *pl.* **-¨** grandmother

grün green

die Gruppe, *pl.* **-n** group

die Gurke, *pl.* **-n** cucumber

der Gürtel, *pl.* **-** belt

gut good; well

H

das Haar, *pl.* **-e** hair

haben, hat, hatte, hat gehabt to have

der Hafen, *pl.* **-¨** harbor

der Haifisch, *pl.* **-** shark

das Hallenbad, *pl.* **-¨er** indoor pool

der Hals, *pl.* **-¨e** neck

die Halskette, *pl.* **-n** necklace

halten, hält, hielt, hat gehalten to stop

die Hand, *pl.* **-¨e** hand

das Handballspiel, *pl.* **-e** game of handball

handeln um to be about

die Harmonie, *pl.* **-n** harmony

hart hard

der Hase, *pl.* **-n** hare

hässlich ugly

die Hauptstraße, *pl.* **-en** main street

das Haus, *pl.* **-¨er** house

die Hausaufgabe, *pl.* **-n** homework

heiß hot

heißen, heißt, hieß, hat geheißen to call oneself

der Held, *pl.* **-en** hero

die Heldin, *pl.* **-nen** heroine

helfen, hilft, half, hat geholfen to help

hellblau light blue

hellgrün light green

das Hemd, *pl.* **-en** shirt

die Henne, *pl.* **-n** hen

her here; ago; toward speaker

herauf up here

heraufkommen, kommt herauf, kam herauf, ist heraufgekommen *sep. prefix* **herauf** to come up (toward speaker)

heraufsteigen, steigt herauf, stieg herauf, ist heraufgestiegen *sep. prefix* **herauf** to climb up (toward speaker)

herausgehen, geht heraus, ging heraus, ist herausgegangen *sep. prefix* come out

herkommen, kommt her, kam her, ist hergekommen *sep. prefix* come here

herlegen *sep. prefix* put down; lay down

herrlich marvelous

heute today

heutzutage nowadays

hier here

die Hilfe, *pl.* **-n** help

hin there; away from speaker

hinaus out there

hinausgehen, geht hinaus, ging hinaus, ist hinausgegangen *sep. prefix* to go out

hinein in there

hineinfahren, fährt hinein, fuhr hinein, ist hineingefahren *sep. prefix* to drive into

hineingehen, geht hinein, ging hinein, ist hineingegangen *sep. prefix* to go into

hineinskaten *sep. prefix* to skate into

hinfahren, fährt hin, fuhr hin, ist hingefahren *sep. prefix* to drive there

die Hinfahrt, en trip to one's destination

hingehen, geht hin, ging hin, ist hingegangen *sep. prefix* to go there

hinlaufen, läuft hin, lief hin, ist hingelaufen *sep. prefix* to run or walk there

hinlegen *sep. prefix* to put down

hinsetzen *sep. prefix* to set down

hinter behind

der Hobbyraum, *pl.* **-¨e** hobby room

hoch high

das Hochhaus, *pl.* **-¨er** high-rise building

hochinteressant highly interesting

hoffen to hope

höher higher

hoppla whoops

die Hose, *pl.* **-n** pants

das Hotel, *pl.* **-s** hotel

hübsch *pl.* pretty

der Hügel, *pl.* **-** hill

die Hühnersuppe, *pl.* **-n** chicken soup

der Hund, *pl.* **-e** dog

der Hunger hunger

der Hustensaft, *pl.* **-¨e** cough syrup

I

ich I

ideal ideal

die Idee, *pl.* **-n** idea

ihn he; it *acc.*

Ihnen to you; you *pol.*

ihr her
im (in + dem) in *dat.*
immer always
in in
der Inhalt, *pl.* **-e** contents
intelligent intelligent
intensiv intensive
interessant interesting
interessieren to interest
das Internet Internet
das Internetcafé, *pl.* **-s** Internet café
das Interview, *pl.* **-s** interview
irgendwo wherever; anywhere

J
ja yes
die Jacke, *pl.* **-n** jacket
das Jahr, *pl.* **-e** year
der Januar, *pl.* **-e** January
die Jeans, - (often used as plural noun) jeans
die Jeanshose, *pl.* **-n** jeans
jeder each; every; (*pl.* **- alle**)
jemand someone
jener that; those
jetzt now
der Job, *pl.* **-s** job
die Jugendherberge, *pl.* **-n** youth hostel
das Jugendhotel, *pl.* **-s** youth hotel
das Jugendzentrum, *pl.* **- zentren** youth center
jung young
der Junge, *pl.* **-n** young man; boy
der Juni, *pl.* **-s** June

K
der Kaffee, *pl.* **-s** coffee
kalt cold
die Kamera, *pl.* **-s** camera
kämmen to comb
kämpfen to fight; to struggle
das Känguru, *pl.* **-s** kangaroo

das Kaninchen, *pl.* **-** rabbit
kaputt broken
die Karte, *pl.* **-n** card
die Kartoffel, *pl.* **-n** potato
das Käsefondue, *pl.* **-s** (*also* **die Käsefondue,** *pl.* **-s**) cheese fondue
die Käseplatte, *pl.* **-n** cheese platter
die Katze, *pl.* **-n** cat
kaufen to buy
das Kaufhaus, *pl.* **-̈er** department store
der Kaufhof, *pl.* **-̈e** department store
kaum hardly
kein no; not any; none
der Keks, *pl.* **-e** cookie
der Kellner, *pl.* **-** waiter
kennen, kennt, kannte, hat gekannt to know (a person or place)
kennenlernen *sep. prefix* **kennen** to meet
das Kind, *pl.* **-er** child
das Kino, *pl.* **-s** movie theater
der Kinobesucher, *pl.* **-** movie patron
der Kiosk, *pl.* **-e** kiosk
die Kirche, *pl.* **-n** church
die Kirschtorte, *pl.* **-n** cherry cake
klar clear; bright
die Klasse, *pl.* **-n** class
der Klassenausflug, *pl.* **-̈e** class trip
der/die Klassenbeste, *pl.* **-n** best student
das Klassenbuch, *pl.* **-̈er** school agenda
die Klassenfahrt, *pl.* **-en** class trip
der Klassenkamerad, *pl.* **-en** classmate
die Klassenliste, *pl.* **-n** class list
klauen to steal (*colloquial*)
das Kleid, *pl.* **-er** dress

das Kleidergeschäft, *pl.* **-e** clothing shop
klein small
die Kleinstadt, *pl.* **-̈e** town
die Kletterwand, *pl.* **-̈e** climbing wall
klingeln to ring
klopfen to knock
klug clever
die Knackwurst, *pl.* **-̈e** knackwurst
knallrot bright red
kochen to cook
die Köchin, *pl.* **-nin** female cook
komisch funny
kommen, kommt, kam, ist gekommen, *v.i.* to come
die Konditorei, *pl.* **-en** café
können, kann, konnte, hat gekonnt to be able to; can
das Konzert, *pl.* **-e** concert
die Konzertkarte, -n concert ticket
der Kopf, *pl.* **-̈e** head
der Korb, *pl.* **-̈e** basket
kosten to cost
der Kranich, *pl.* **-e** crane
krank sick
das Krankenhaus, *pl.* **-̈er** hospital
der Krankenwagen, *pl.* **-** ambulance
kratzen to scratch
die Krawatte, *pl.* **-n** necktie
kreativ creative
kriechen, kriecht, kroch, ist gekrochen to crawl
kriegen to get (*colloquial*)
der Kriminalroman, *pl.* **-e** detective novel
das Krokodil, -e crocodile
die Küche, *pl.* **-n** kitchen
der Kuchen, *pl.* **-** cake
der Kuchenteller, *pl.* **-** cake plate
die Kuckucksuhr, *pl.* **-en** cuckoo clock
der Kuli, *pl.* **-s** ballpoint pen

kurz short
das Kuscheltier, *pl.* **-e** stuffed animal

L
der Laden, *pl.* **-** shop
das Lagerfeuer, *pl.* **-** campfire
die Lampe, *pl.* **-n** lamp
das Land, *pl.* **-er** country
die Landkarte, *pl.* **-n** map
lang long
langsam slow
lästig bothersome; cumbersome
der Lastwagen, *pl.* **-** truck
laufen, läuft, lief, ist gelaufen, *v.i.* to run
laut loud
leben to live
das Leben, *pl.* **-** life
die Lebensgeschichte, *pl.* **-n** life story
das Lebensmittel, *pl.* **-** food, groceries
lecker tasty
das Leder, *pl.* **-** leather
die Lederjacke, *pl.* **-en** leather jacket
leer empty
legen to lay; to place
der Lehrer, *pl.* **-** male teacher
die Lehrerin, *pl.* **-nen** female teacher
leicht light
das Leid sorrow
leiden to suffer
leiden an + *acc.* to suffer from
leider unfortunately
lernen to learn
das Lernen learning
lesen, liest, las, hat gelesen, *v.t.* to read
lesenswert worthy of reading
letzter last
die Leute, *pl.* people
lieb dear; nice

lieber *adv.* preferably
das Lied, *pl.* **-er** song
liegen, liegt, lag, hat gelegen to be situated; lie
die Limo, *pl.* **-s** soda
links left; to the left
die Liste, *pl.* **-n** list
das Literatengespräch, *pl.* **-e** literary discussion
das Loch, *pl.* **-er** hole
löschen to put out; to delete
lustig funny

M
machen to make; to do
das Mädchen, *pl.* **-** girl
der Magier, *pl.* **-** magician
mähen to mow
der Mai, *pl.* **-e** May
das Make-up, *pl.* **-s** makeup
mal time; once
man one
mancher some
der Mann, *pl.* **-er** man
die Mannschaft, *pl.* **-en** team
der Mantel, *pl.* **-** coat
der Marathonlauf, *pl.* **-e** marathon
der Markplatz, *pl.* **-** marketplace
die Marktstraße, *pl.* **-n** market street
die Mathe math
der Mathelehrer, *pl.* **-** male math teacher
die Maus, *pl.* **-e** mouse
das Meer, *pl.* **-e** sea
mehr more
mein my
die Meinung, *pl.* **-en** opinion
meistens most of the time
merken to notice
das Messer, *pl.* **-** knife
die Metzgerei, *pl.* **-n** butcher shop
der Millionär, *pl.* **-e** millionaire

der Mini-Bierkrug, *pl.* **-e** mini beer stein
die Minute, *pl.* **-n** minute
mir to me
mislingen, mislingt, mislang, ist mislungen to fail
das Missverständnis, *pl.* **-e** misunderstanding
mit with
mitbringen, bringt mit, brachte mit, hat mitgebracht *sep. prefix* to bring with
mitfahren fährt mit, fuhr mit, ist mitgefahren *sep. prefix* to travel with
mitgehen, geht mit, ging mit, ist mitgegangen *sep. prefix* to go with; to go along
mitkommen, kommt mit, kam mit, ist mitgekommen *sep. prefix* to come with; to come along
mitnehmen, nimmt mit, nahm mit, hat mitgenommen *sep. prefix* to take with; to take along
der Mittag, *pl.* **-e** noon
das Mittagsbrot, *pl.* **-e** lunch
das Mittagsschläfchen, *pl.* **-** afternoon nap
mittelalterlich medieval
die Mitternacht, *pl.* **-e** midnight
die Mode, *pl.* **-n** style; fashion
modern modern
modisch stylish; fashionable
mögen, mag, mochte, hat gemocht to like to
die Möglichkeit, *pl.* **-en** possibility
möglich possible
möglicherweise possibly
der/das Moment, *pl.* **-e** moment

der Monat, *pl.* **-e** month
der Montag, *pl.* **-e** Monday
montags on Mondays
der Morgen, *pl.* **-** morning
morgen tomorrow
morge früh tomorrow morning
morgens in the morning
das Mosaik, *pl.* **-en** mosaic
das Motorrad, *pl.* **-̈er** motorcyle
das Motorskateboard, *pl.* **-s** motorized skateboard
das Murmeltier, *pl.* **-e** groundhog
das Museum, die Museen museum
der Museumsdirektor, *pl.* **-en** museum director
der Museumsführer, *pl.* **-** museum guide
musikalisch musical
der Muskel, *pl.* **-n** muscle
müssen, muss, musste, hat gemusst to have to; must
die Mutter, *pl.* **-̈** mother
die Mutti, *pl.* **-s** mom; mommy

N
nach after
nachdem afterwards
nachkommen, kommt nach, kam nach, ist nachgekommen *sep. prefix* to come later; to follow
der Nachmittag, *pl.* **-e** afternoon
nachmittags in the afternoon
nächster next
die Nacht, *pl.* **-̈** night
nachts at night
nagelneu brand new
die Nähe, *pl.* **-en** vicinity
der Name, *pl.* **-n** name
nass wet
natürlich naturally

neben nearby; next to
der Neffe, *pl.* **-n** nephew
nehmen, nimmt, nahm, hat genommen to take
nein no
nennen, nennt, nannte, hat genannt to name
nett nice
neu new; young
neugotisch neogothic
nicht not
der Nichtraucher, *pl.* **-** non-smoker
nichts nothing
nie never
niemand no one
das Nilpferd, *pl.* **-e** hippopotamus
noch still
normal normal
normalerweise normally
die Note, *pl.* **-n** mark, grade
das Notebook, *pl.* **-s** laptop computer
nötig necessary
die Nummer, *pl.* **-n** number
nun now
nur only
nützlich useful

O
ob if; whether
das Obst fruit
obwohl although
oder or
öffnen, *v.t.* to open
oft often
ohne without
das Ohr, *pl.* **-en** ear
olympisch olympic
die Oma, *pl.* **-s** grandma
der Opa, *pl.* **-s** grandpa
der Onkel, *pl.* **-** uncle
die Oper, *pl.* **-n** opera
ordnen to order
die Ordnung, *pl.* **-en** order
die Organization, *pl.* **-en** organization

der Orangensaft, *pl.* **-̈e** orange juice
das Österreich Austria
der Ozean, *pl.* **-e** ocean

P
packen to pack
der Packzettel, *pl.* **-** packing slip
der Park, -s park
das Parkhaus, *pl.* **-̈er** multi-story parking lot
der Partner, *pl.* **-** partner
passen to fit
passieren to happen
die Pause, *pl.* **-n** break
peinlich embarassing
die Persönlichkeit, *pl.* **-en** personality
der Pfau, *pl.* **-e** peacock
pfeifen, pfeift, pfiff, hat gepfiffen to whistle
das Pferd, *pl.* **-e** horse
das Pferdereiten horseback riding
der Pfingstmontag, *pl.* **-e** Whit Monday, Pentecost Monday
die Pfingstferien *pl.* Pentecost vacation
pflücken to pick
der Picknickkorb, *pl.* **-̈e** picnic basket
die Pizza, *pl.* **-s** or **die Pizzen** pizza
das Plakat, *pl.* **-e** poster
der Plan, *pl.* **-̈e** plan
das Plurallied, *pl.* **-er** Song about noun plurals
polieren to polish
der Politiker, *pl.* **-** politician
die Polizei police
der Polizist, *pl.* **-en** policeman
die Pommes frites, *pl.* French fries
die Post mail
das Postamt, *pl.* **-̈er** post office

der Postbus, *pl.* **-se** public bus used to carry passengers and mail in rural areas

das Poster, *pl.* **-** poster

die Postkarte, *pl.* **-n** postcard

prächtig splendid

prachtvoll magnificent

probieren to try

das Problem, *pl.* **-e** problem

die Professorin, *pl.* **-nen** female professor

der Pulli, *pl.* **-s** pullover sweater

putzen to clean

R

das Rad, *pl.* **-¨er** bike

die Radtour, *pl.* **-en** bike tour

der Rasen, *pl.* **-** lawn

rasieren to shave

das Rathaus, *pl.* **-¨er** town hall

die Ratte, *pl.* **-n** rat

rauchen to smoke

der Raucher, *pl.* **-** smoker

recht right (*direction*)

rechts to the right

reden to speak

das Regal, *pl.* **-e** set of shelves

der Regenmantel, *pl.* **-¨** raincoat

der Regenschirm, *pl.* **-e** umbrella

regnen to rain

regnerisch rainy

die Reihe, *pl.* **-en** row

reinkommen, kommt rein, kam rein, ist reingekommen *sep. prefix* to enter; to come in

die Reise, *pl.* **-n** trip

das Reisebuch, *pl.* **-¨er** travel journal

die Reisetasche, *pl.* **-en** travel bag

reiten, reiten, ritt, ist/hat geritten to ride (*an animal*)

rennen, rennt, rannte, ist gerannt to run

reservieren to reserve

das Restaurant, *pl.* **-s** restaurant

das Rezept, *pl.* **-e** prescription

richtig correct, right

riechen, reicht, roch, hat gerochen to smell

riesig huge; enormous

die Rockmusik rock music

der Roller, *pl.* **-** scooter

der Roman, *pl.* **-e** novel

die Rose, *pl.* **-en** rose

rot red

die Routine, *pl.* **-n** routine

der Rucksack, *pl.* **-¨e** knapsack

das Ruderboot, *pl.* **-e** rowboat

rudern to row

rülpsen to belch, burp

S

sagen to say

der Salat, -e salad

der Samstag, *pl.* **-e** Saturday

die Sandkiste, *pl.* **-n** sandbox

sauber clean

sauer sour

das Schach chess

das Schachturnier, *pl.* **-e** chess tournament

schade too bad

schaden to spoil, to damage; to harm

schädlich harmful

der Schäferhund, *pl.* **-e** German shepard

der Schal, *pl.* **-e** scarf

scharf sharp

schauen to look

schaufeln to shovel

schick chic

schicken to send

die Schildkröte, *pl.* **-n** turtle

das Schillerbuch, *pl.* **-¨er** Schiller book

das Schillerposter, *pl.* **-s/-** Schiller poster

Schillerstraße, *pl.* **-n** Schiller Street

die Schilleruhr, *pl.* **-en** Schiller clock

der Schirm, *pl.* **-e** umbrella

der Schiwettbewerb, *pl.* **-e** ski competition

schlafen, schläft, schlief, hat geschlafen to sleep

der Schlafsack, *pl.* **-¨e** sleeping bag

schlagen, schlägt, schlug, hat geschlagen *pl.* to hit; to beat

die Schlagsahne, *pl.* **-n** whipped cream

schlampig sloppy

die Schlange, *pl.* **-n** snake

schlank thin

schlecht bad

schleichen to slink

schließen, schließt, schloss, hat geschlossen to close; to end

schließlich finally

das Schloss, *pl.* **-¨er** castle

schmecken to taste

der Schmetterling, *pl.* **-e** butterfly

die Schminke, *pl.* **-n** makeup

schminken to put on makeup

der Schmuck jewelry

schmutzig dirty

der Schnee snow

schnell fast

der Schnellimbiss, *pl.* **-e** fast food restaurant

schon already

schön beautiful

schreiben, schreibt, schrieb, hat geschrieben, *v.t., pl.* to write

das Schreibwarengeschäft, *pl.* **-e** stationery store

der Schuh, *pl.* **-e** shoe

die Schule, *pl.* **-n** school

der Schüler, *pl.* - male student

der Schülerausweis, *pl.* **-e** student id

die Schülerin, *pl.* **-nen** female student

die Schulklasse, *pl.* **-n** class; grade

der Schultag, *pl.* **-e** school day

die Schultasche, *pl.* **-n** school bag

schwäbisch Swabian

schwarz black

der Schwarzwald Black Forest

das Schweizer Messer, *pl.* - Swiss Army knife

schwer difficult

die Schwester, *pl.* **-n** sister

das Schwimmbad, *pl.* **-̈er** swimming pool

schwimmen, schwimmt, schwamm, ist/hat geschwommen, *v.i.* to swim

das Schwimmen swimming

die Schwimmhalle, *pl.* **-n** indoor swimming pool

der Sechsklässler, *pl.* - sixth grader

der See, *pl.* **-n** lake

die See, *pl.* **-n** sea

sehen, sieht, sah, hat gesehen to see

die Sehenswürdigkeit, *pl.* **-en** sight; tourist attraction

sehr very

sein, ist, war, ist gewesen, *v.i.* to be

seit since

die Seite, *v.i.* **-n** side

die Selbstbeschreibung, -en description of oneself

selbstgebacken home baked

selbstverständlich of course

selten often

der September, *pl.* - September

servieren to serve

die Serviette, *pl.* **-n** napkin

der Sessel, *pl.* - arm chair

setzen to set

die Shorts, *pl.* shorts

sich ärgern über + *acc.* to get angry

sich anziehen, zieht sich an, zog sich an, hat sich angezogen to get dressed

sich ausziehen, zieht sich aus, zog sich aus, hat sich ausgezogen to get dressed

sich beeilen hurry

sich bemühen um +*acc.* to try

sich benenhmen, benimmt sich, benahm sich, hat sich benommen to behave (*oneself*)

sich beschäftigen mit + *dat.* to occupy oneself

sich bewerben um + *acc.* to apply for

sich blamieren to embarrass oneself

sich freuen auf + *acc.* to look forward to

sich freuen über + *acc.* to become happy about

sich gewöhnen an + *acc.* to get used to

sich handeln um + *acc.* to be about

sich interessieren für + *acc.* to be interested

sich irren to make a mistake, err

sich kämmen (also sich) *dat.* **die Haare kämmen)** to comb one's hair

sich schämen to be ashamed

sich sorgen um + *acc.* to worry about

sich verlassen auf + *acc.* to depend on

sich verlieben in + *acc.* to fall in love with

sicher sure

sie she, it *fem.*, they

Sie you *pol.*

sieben seven

der Siebtklässler, *pl.* - seventh grader

der Silberschmuck silver jewelry

singen, singt, sang, hat gesungen to sing

sitzen, sitzt, saß, hat gesessen to sit

der Skater, *pl.* - skater

so thus

die Socke, *pl.* **-n** sock

sofort immediately

der Sohn, *pl.* **-̈e** son

solcher such

sollen, soll, sollte, hat gesollt to be supposed to; should

der Sommer, *pl.* - summer

die Sommerferien, *pl.* summer vacation

sondern rather

die Sonne, *pl.* **-n** sun

der Sonnenschein sunshine

der Sonntag, -e Sunday

die Sonntagshose, *pl.* **-n** Sunday pants

sorgen für + *acc.* to look after; to care for

sowieso anyway

das Spanisch Spanish

der Spaß, *pl.* **-̈e** fun; joke

spät late

später later

spazieren (ist spaziert) to walk, to take a walk

die Speisekarte, *pl.* **-n** menu

das Spiel, *pl.* **-e** game

spielen, *v.t.* to play

das Spielen playing

der Spieler, - player

die Spielkarte, *pl.* **-n** playing card

der Spielplatz, *pl.* **-̈e** playground

das Spielzeug, *pl.* **-e** toy

der Spinat, *pl.* **-e** spinach

der **Sport**, *pl.* -e sports
die **Sportabteilung**, *pl.* -en sports department
das **Sportgeschäft**, *pl.* -e sporting good store
die **Sporthalle**, *pl.* -n gymnasium
die **Sportkleider** athletic clothing
der **Sportladen**, *pl.* -¨ sporting goods store
der **Sportler**, - athlete
sportlich sporty
der **Sportplatz**, *pl.* -¨e athletic field
das **Sprachfest**, *pl.* -e
sprechen, spricht, sprach, hat gesprochen to speak
der **Springbrunnen**, *pl.* - fountain
springen, springt, sprang, ist gesprungen to jump
das **Stadion, die Stadien** stadium
die **Stadt**, *pl.* -¨e city
der **Stadtführer**, *pl.* - city guide
die **Stadthalle**, *pl.* -n city hall
die **Stadtkapelle**, *pl.* -n city or town orchestra
der **Stadtpark**, *pl.* -s city park
der **Stadtplan**, *pl.* -¨e city map
die **Stadtsgallerie**, *pl.* -n city gallery
der **Stadttag**, *pl.* -e day in the city
das **Stadttheater**, *pl.* - city theater
die **Stadttour**, *pl.* -en city tour
stark strong
der **Startpunkt**, *pl.* -e starting point
staubsaugen, staubsaugt, staubsaugte, hat staubgesaugt to vacuum
stecken to stick
stehen, steht, stand, hat gestanden to stand

stehlen, stiehlt, stahl, hat gestohlen to steal; to crawl
steigen, steigt, stieg, ist gestiegen to climb
stellen to place
sterben, stirbt, starb, ist gestorben, *v.i.* to die
die **Stereoanlage**, *pl.* -en stereo system
still still, quiet
der **Storch**, *pl.* -¨e stork
der **Strand**, *pl.* -¨e beach
die **Straße**, *pl.* -n street
die **Straßenbahn**, *pl.* -en streetcar; trolley
die **Straßenlampe**, *pl.* -en streetlamp
streng strict
stricken to knit
strömen to stream; flow
der **Strumpf**, *pl.* -¨e stocking
das **Stück**, *pl.* -e piece
der **Student**, *pl.* -en male student
studieren, *v.t.* enrolled at a college or university
die **Stunde**, *pl.* -en hour
super super
der **Supermarkt**, *pl.* -¨e supermarket
süß sweet
die **Süßigkeit**, *pl.* -en candy, sweet

T

der **Tag**, *pl.* -e day
das **Tagebuch**, *pl.* -¨er diary
täglich daily
das **Tal**, *pl.* -¨er valley
die **Tankstelle**, *pl.* -n gas station
die **Tante**, *pl.* -n aunt
die **Tasche**, *pl.* -n pocket; bag
die **Taschenlampe**, *pl.* -n flashlight
die **Taschenuhr**, *pl.* -en pocket watch
die **Tasse**, *pl.* -n cup

die **Taube**, *pl.* -n pigeon, dove
die **Tauchbrille**, *pl.* -n diving mask
tauchen dive; to dip
tausend thousand
das **Taxi**, *pl.* -s taxi
das **Team**, *pl.* -s team
der **Teddybär**, *pl.* -en Teddy bear
der **Tee**, *pl.* -s tea
teilen to share
teilnehmen an + *dat*, **nimmt teil, nahm teil, hat teilgenommen** *sep. prefix* to take part in; to participate in
teilweise partly
der **Telefonanruf**, *pl.* -e telephone call
telefonieren mit + *dat, v.t.* to speak to s.o. on the telephone
der **Teller**, *pl.* - plate
der **Tennisball**, *pl.* -¨e tennis ball
der **Tennischuh**, *pl.* -e sneaker
der **Tennistrainer**, *pl.* - tennis coach
testen to test
teuer expensive
das **Theater**, *pl.* - theater
die **Theaterkarte**, *pl.* -n theater ticket
tief deep
das **Tier**, *pl.* -e animal
die **Tiergeschichte**, *pl.* -n animal story
die **Tierhandlung**, *pl.* -en pet shop
der **Tierpark**, *pl.* -s zoo
der **Tisch**, -e table
die **Tischdecke**, *pl.* -n tablecloth
die **Tochter**, *pl.* -¨ daughter
toll great; amazing
dir **Torte**, *pl.* -n cake
die **Tour**, *pl.* -en tour
der **Tourist**, *pl.* -en tourist

der Tourleiter, *pl.* - tour guide

tragen, trägt, trug, hat getragen *v.t.* to wear; to carry

trainieren to train

das Training, *pl.* **-s** training

die Traube, *pl.* **-n** grape

traurig sad

treu faithful

trinken, trinkt, trank, hat getrunken, *v.t.* to drink

der Trompetenspieler, *pl.* - trumpet player

das T-Shirt, *pl.* **-s** T-shirt

tun, tut, tat, hat getan to do

der Tunnel, *pl.* - tunnel

die Tür, *pl.* **-en** door

die Türmatte, *pl.* **-n** doormat

der Typ, *pl.* **-en** guy; type

U

die U-Bahn, *pl.* **-en** subway

überall everywhere

übermorgen day after tomorrow

übernachten to stay overnight

die Übung, *pl.* **-en** lesson

die Uhr, *pl.* **-en** clock

um at

die Umfrage, *pl.* **-n** interview; survey

und and

unfair unfair

ungerecht unfair

ungern reluctant

unglücklich unhappy, unlucky

unheimlich eerie; creepy; terrific

die Uni, *pl.* **-s** university

unlesbar illegible

unmöglich impossible

unrecht wrong

uns useful

unser our

unter under

die Untertasse, *pl.* **-n** saucer

unterwegs on the way

unvorbereitet unprepared

unzufrieden dissatisfied

der Urlaub, *pl.* **-s** trip

V

der Vater, *pl.* -¨ father

der Vati, *pl.* **-s** dad; daddy

verdienen to earn

die Vergangenheit, *pl.* **-en** past

vergessen, vergisst, vergaß, hat vergessen to forget

der Vergleich, *pl.* **-e** comparison

die Verhandlung, *pl.* **-en** negotiation

die Verkäuferin, *pl.* **-nen** salesgirl

das Verkehrsschild, *pl.* **-er** traffic sign

verlassen auf + *acc.* to rely upon

verlieren, verliert, verlor, hat verloren to lose

verloren lost

verpassen to miss

die Versicherung, *pl.* **-en** insurance

verstehen, versteht, verstand, hat verstanden understand

der/die Verwandte, *pl.* **-n** relative

verzaubert bewitched

verzeihen, verzeiht, verzieh, hat verzogen to forgive

verzichten auf + *acc.* to do without; to pass up

der Video-Ablaufplan, *pl.* -¨e story board

die Videogeschichte, *pl.* **-n** video storyboard

die Videokamera, *pl.* **-s** video camera

viel much

viele many

vielleicht perhaps

vier four

der Vogel, *pl.* -¨ bird

das Volkslied, *pl.* **-er** folksong

die Volksmusik folk music

völlig complete

vom (von + dem) from the, of the

von *prep. dat.* from; of

vor before; in front of

die Vorbereitung, *pl.* **-en** preparation

vorgestern day before yesterday

vorhaben, hat vor, hatte vor, hat vorgehabt to have planned

vorher beforehand

vorlesen, liest vor, las vor, hat vorgelesen to read aloud

vorsichtig careful

der Vorsprung, *pl.* -¨e advantage, leap forward

vorstellen *sep. prefix* introduce

W

wachsen, wächst, wuchs, bin gewachsen to grow

der Wagen, *pl.* - car

wählen to choose

wahr true

während while; during

wahrscheinlich probably

der Wald, *pl.* -¨er forest

der Waldweg, *pl.* **-e** forest path

die Wand, *pl.* -¨e wall

die Wanderhose, *pl.* **-n** hiking pants

die Wandermöglichkeit, *pl.* **-en** hiking opportunity

wandern to hike

das Wandern hiking

der Wanderschuh, *pl.* **-e** hiking shoe

der Wanderstiefel, *pl.* - hiking boot

der Wanderstock, *pl.* -¨e hiking stick

der Wanderweg, *pl.* -e hiking trail

wann wann

war was

warm warm

warten, *v.t.* to wait

warten auf + *acc.* to wait for

das Wartezimmer, *pl.* - waiting room

warum why

was what

die Wäsche, *pl.* -n wash laundry

waschen, wäscht, wusch, hat geswachen to wash

wasserdicht watertight

der Weg, *pl.* -e path

weggehen, geht weg, ging weg, ist weggegangen *sep. prefix* to go away

wegstellen *sep. prefix* to put away

wehtun, tut weh, tat weh, hat wehgetan *sep. prefix* to do harm; to hurt

weil because

weinen to cry

weiß white; knows

die Weißwurst, *pl.* -¨e veal sausage

weit wide

welcher which

wem whom, to/for/from whom

wen whom

wenig a little

wenige a few

wenn when; whenever, if

wer who

werden, wird, wurde, ist geworden to become; will

werfen, wirft, warf, hat geworfen to throw

wertvoll valuable

der Wettbewerb, *pl.* -e competition

das Wetter, *pl.* - weather

die Wettervohersage, *pl.* -n weather forecast

wie how

wieder again

die Wiese, *pl.* -n meadow

der Winterschal, *pl.* -e winter scarf

wir we

wissen, weiß, wusste, hat gewusst to know (*a fact*)

wo where

die Woche, *pl.* -n week

das Wochenende, *pl.* -n weekend

wochenlang week-long

wohnen to live

das Wohnhaus, *pl.* -¨er apartment building

die Wohnung, *pl.* -en apartment

das Wohnzimmer, *pl.* - living room

der Wolf, *pl.* -¨e wolf

wollen, will, wollte, hat gewollt to want to; to want

die Wortschatzliste, *pl.* -n vocabulary list

wovon from where, of what

die Wunschliste, *pl.* -n wishlist

wünschen to wish

würde would

die Wurst, *pl.* -¨e sausage; coldcuts

das Wurstbrot, *pl.* -e sausage or coldcut sandwich

die Wurstplatte, *pl.* -n sausage or coldcut platter

die Wüste, *pl.* -n desert

wütend furious

Z

der Zahn, *pl.* -¨e tooth

zehn ten

zeigen to show

die Zeit, *pl.* -en time

die Zeitung, *pl.* -en newspaper

zelten to go camping in tents

das Zimmer, *pl.* - bedroom

zitieren to quote

der Zoo, *pl.* -s zoo

zu to; too; toward

zu zweit in pairs

zuerst first of all

zuhören, *v.t., sep. prefix* to listen to

die Zukunft, *pl.* -¨e future

der Zukunftsplan, *pl.* -¨e future plan

zum (zu + dem) to the

zumachen *sep. prefix* to close

zur (zu + der) to the

zurückfahren, fährt zurück, fuhr zurück, ist zurückgefahren *sep. prefix* to drive back

zurück back

zurückgehen, geht zurück, ging zurück, ist zurückgegangen *sep. prefix* to go back

zurückkommen, kommt zurück, kam zurück, ist zurückgekommen *sep. prefix* to come back

zusammen together

zusammenbleiben, bleibt zusammen, blieb zusammen, ist zusammengeblieben *sep. prefix* to stay together

zusammenstellen *sep. prefix* **zusammen** to put together

zwei two

zweifeln an + *acc.* to have doubts about

zweit second

der Zwilling, -en twins

zwischen between

zwölf twelve